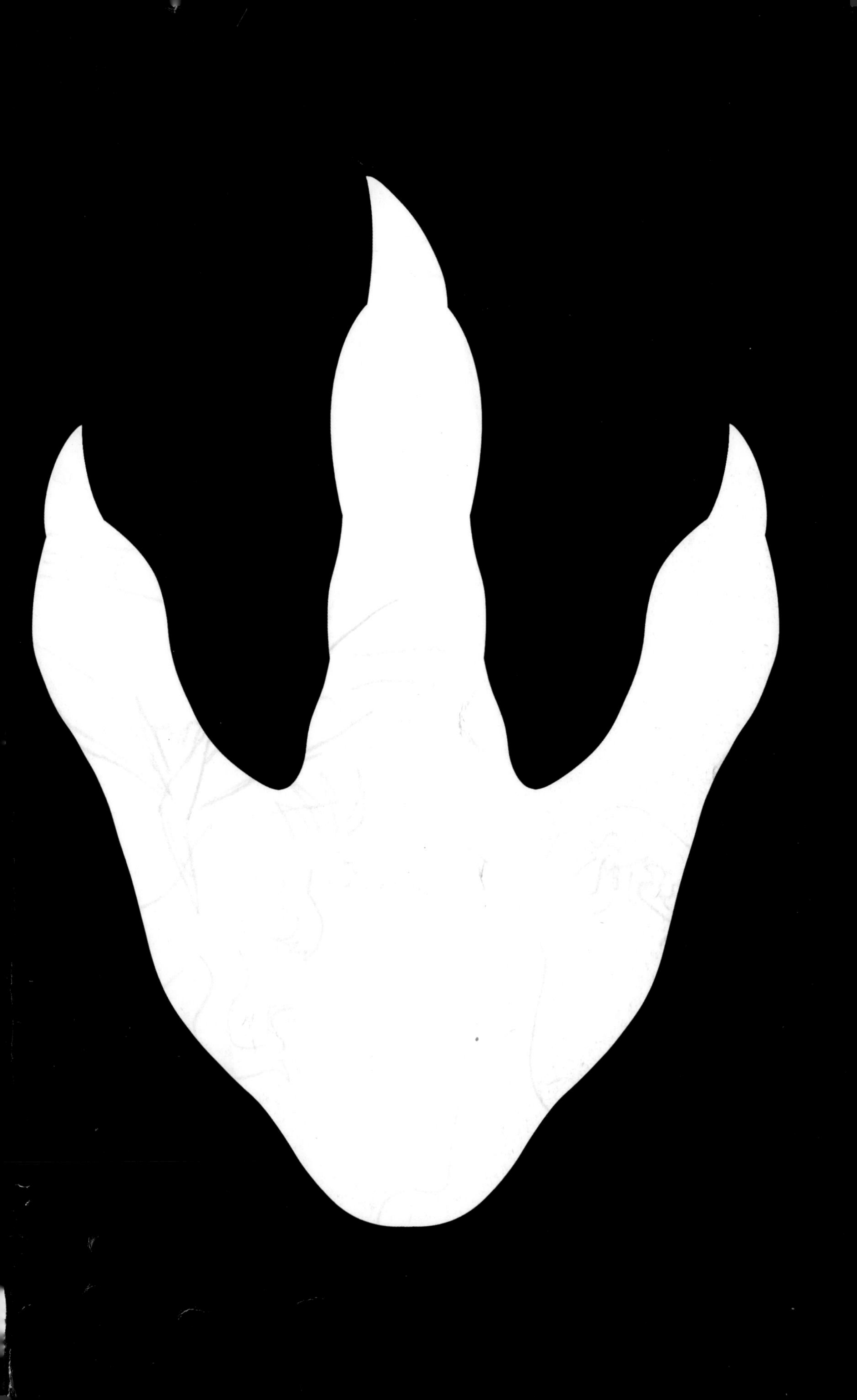

REXTOOTH STUDIOS

JURASSIC

WRITTEN & ILLUSTRATED BY TED RECHLIN

EDITOR

ANNE RECHLIN

COPYRIGHT © 2017 BY TED RECHLIN

PUBLISHED BY REXTOOTH STUDIOS, BOZEMAN, MONTANA

PRODUCED BY SWEETGRASS BOOKS, HELENA, MONTANA

ISBN: 978-1-59152-202-7

COVER DESIGN BY TED RECHLIN

PRODUCED IN THE UNITED STATES OF AMERICA

PRINTED IN CHINA

FOR DECADES **BRONTOSAURUS** WAS THOUGHT TO HAVE NEVER EXISTED, THAT ITS BONES BELONGED TO ANOTHER DINOSAUR - **APATOSAURUS**.

IN 2015 THE WORLD OF DINOSAUR SCIENCE WAS ROCKED BY A **THUNDERBOLT**. THOSE BONES DID NOT COME FROM APATOSAURUS AFTER ALL.

THE BRONTOSAURUS IS **BACK**.

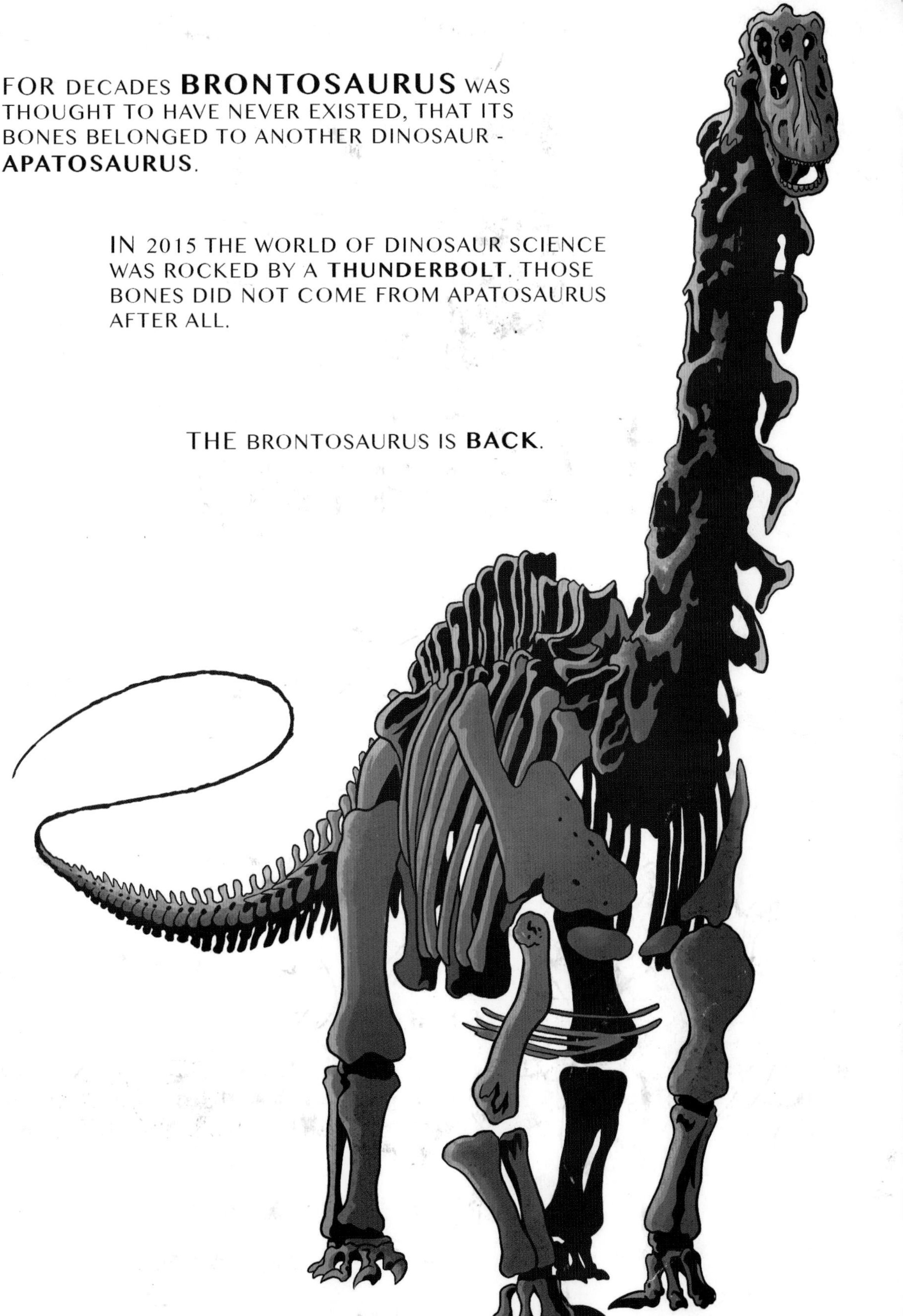

THE **THUNDER LIZARD** HAS RETURNED.

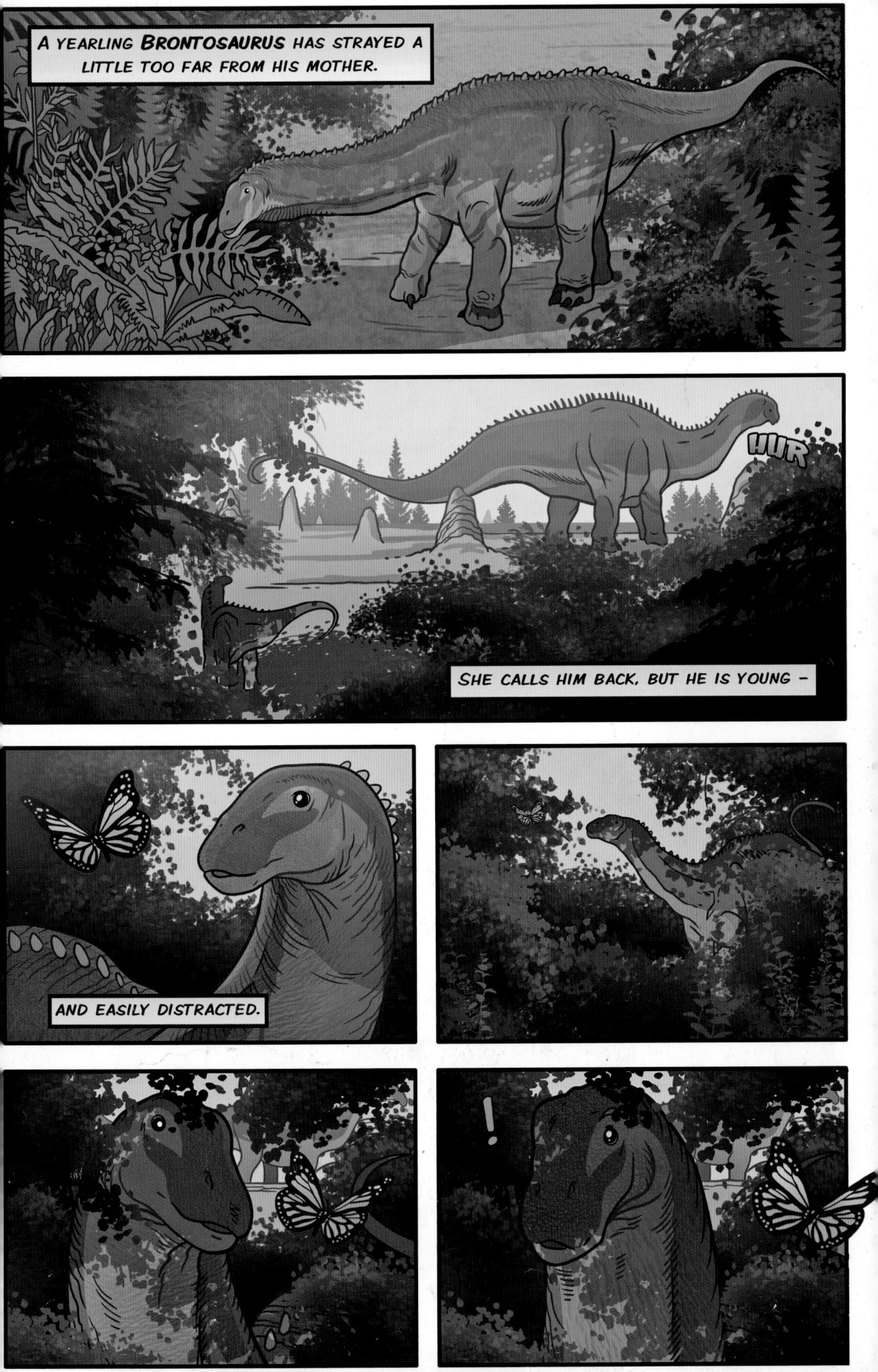
A YEARLING BRONTOSAURUS HAS STRAYED A LITTLE TOO FAR FROM HIS MOTHER.
HUR
SHE CALLS HIM BACK, BUT HE IS YOUNG –
AND EASILY DISTRACTED.
!

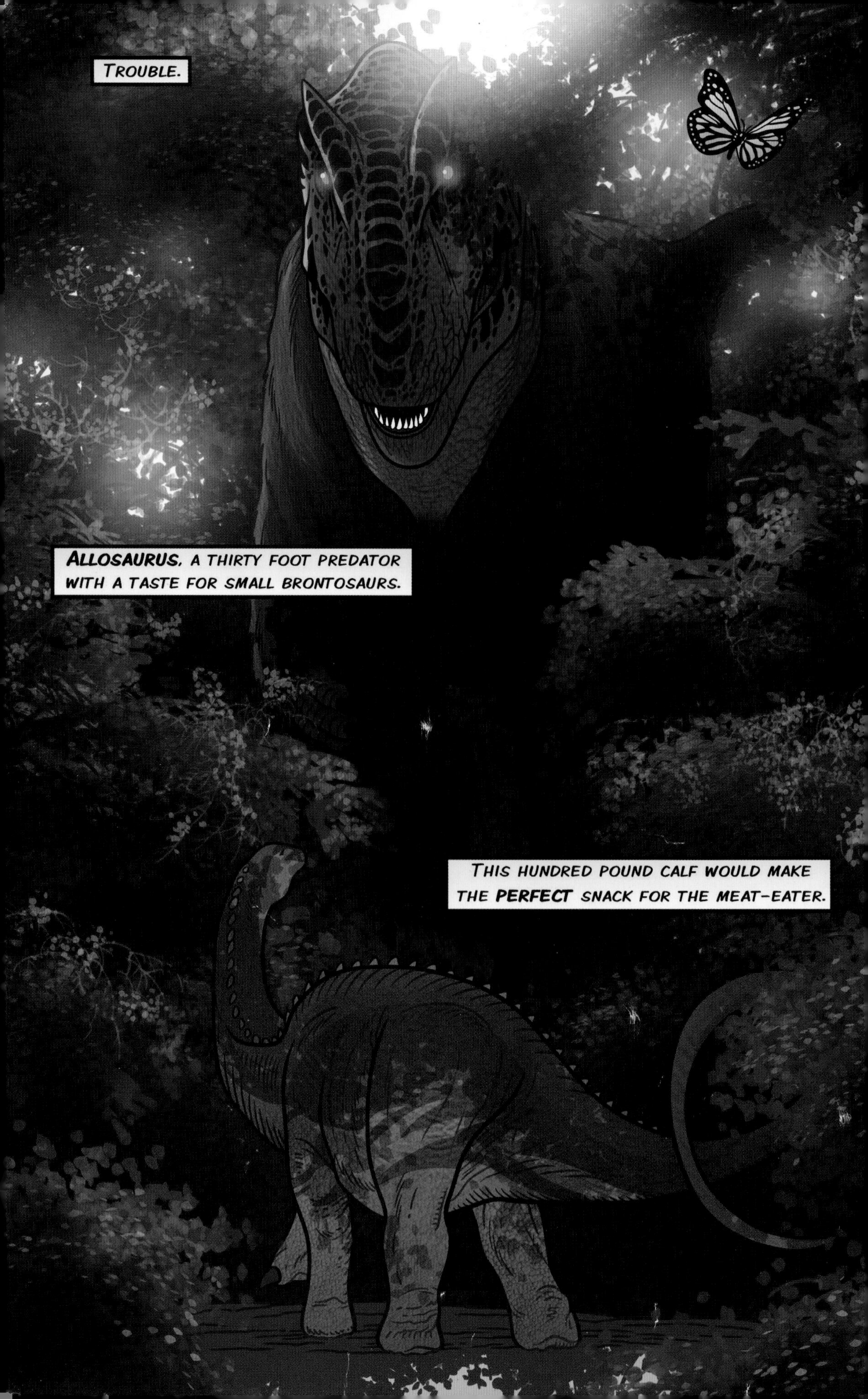
TROUBLE.
ALLOSAURUS, A THIRTY FOOT PREDATOR WITH A TASTE FOR SMALL BRONTOSAURS.
THIS HUNDRED POUND CALF WOULD MAKE THE PERFECT SNACK FOR THE MEAT-EATER.

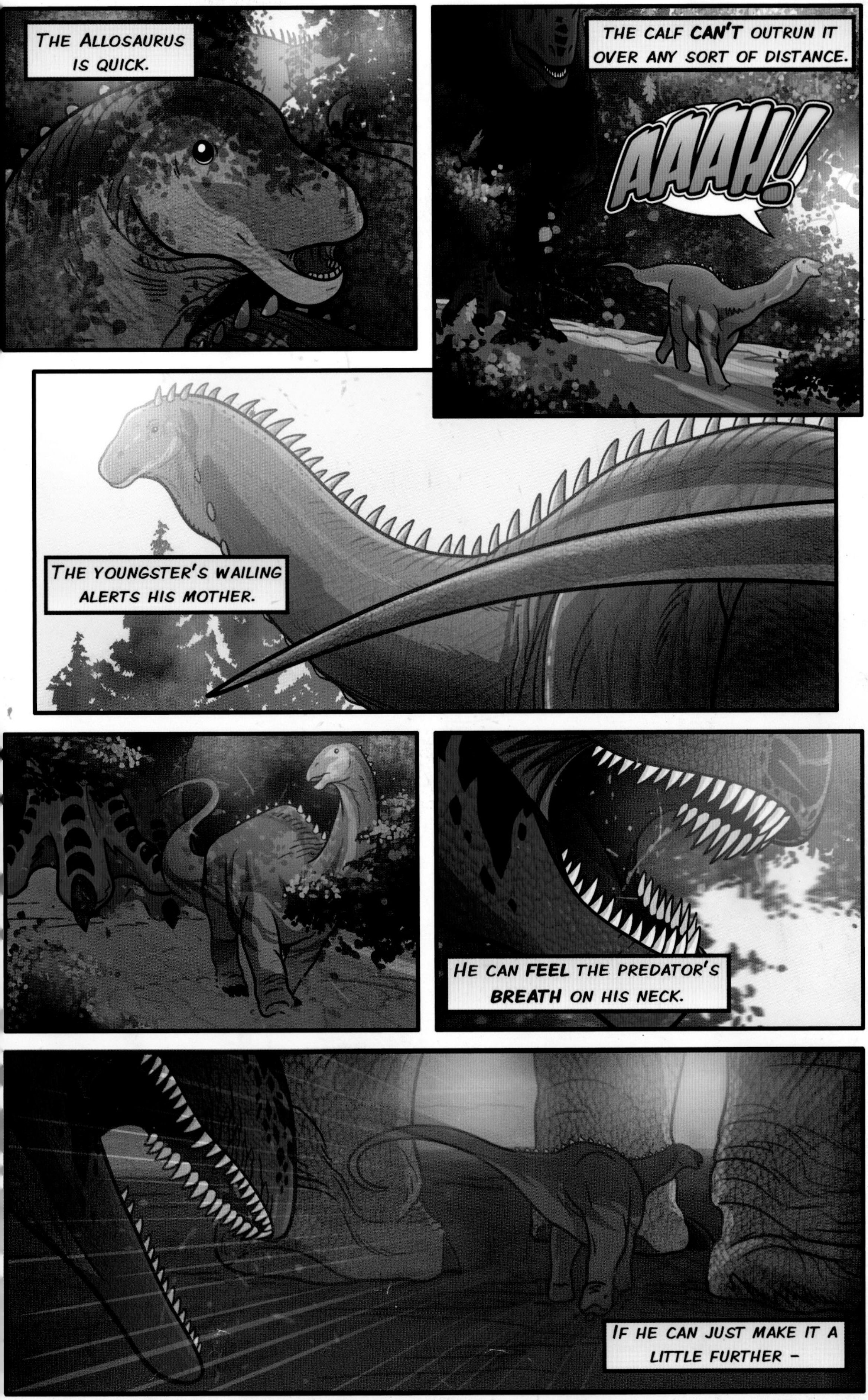
THE ALLOSAURUS IS QUICK.
THE CALF CAN'T OUTRUN IT OVER ANY SORT OF DISTANCE.
AAAH!!
THE YOUNGSTER'S WAILING ALERTS HIS MOTHER.
HE CAN FEEL THE PREDATOR'S BREATH ON HIS NECK.
IF HE CAN JUST MAKE IT A LITTLE FURTHER –

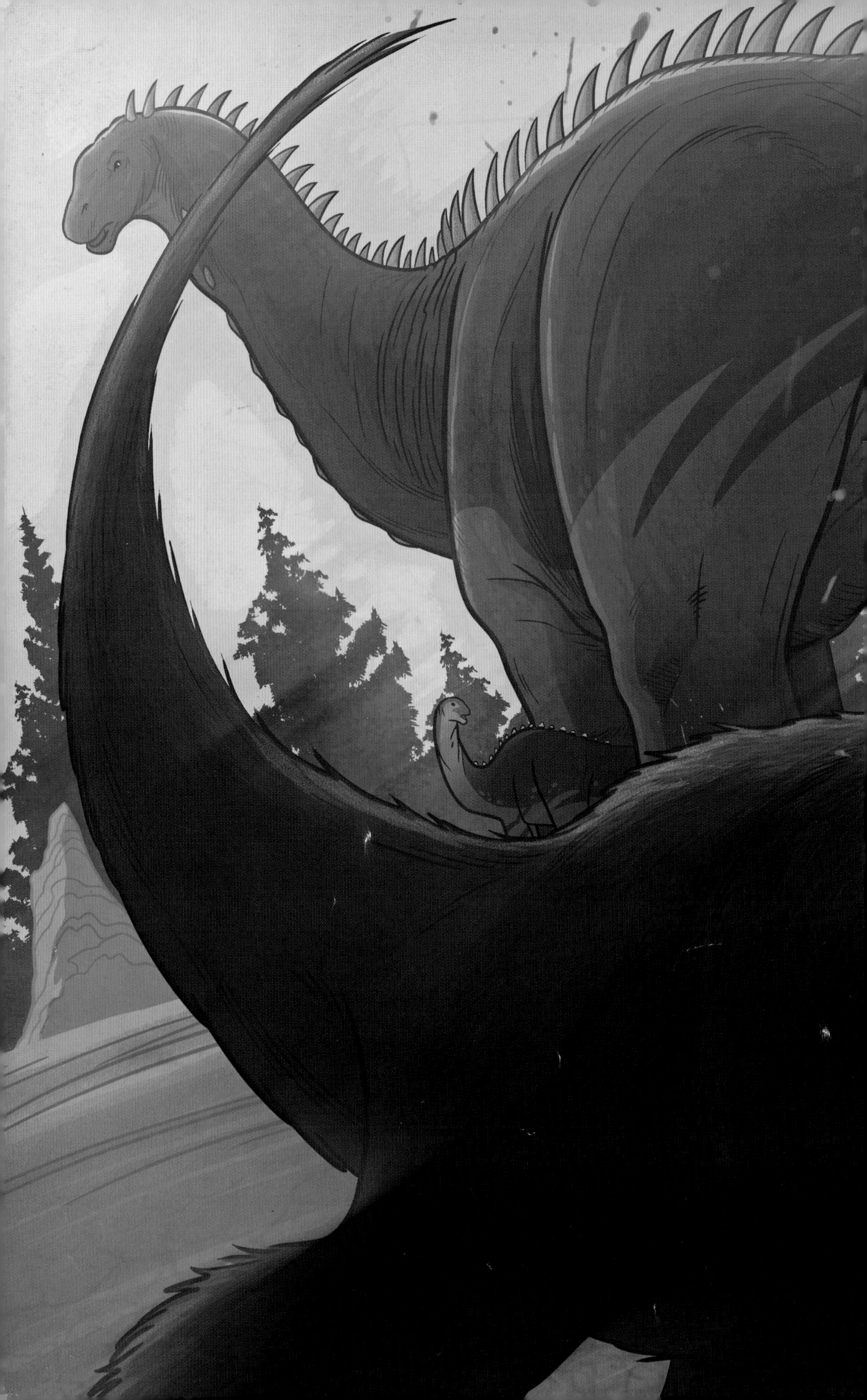

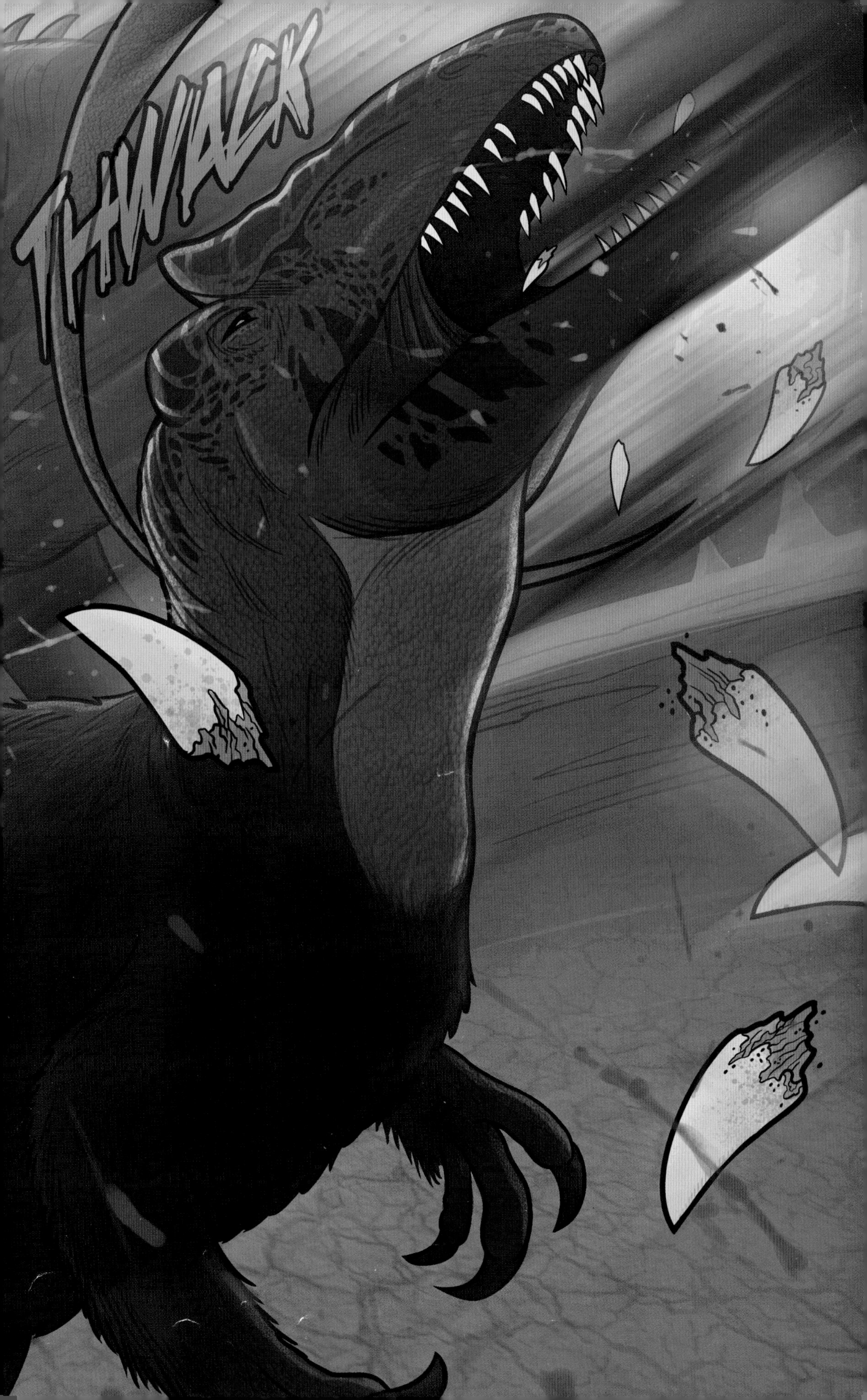
THWACK

JURASSIC

WRITTEN & ILLUSTRATED BY
TED RECHLIN
PRESENTED BY
REXTOOTH STUDIOS

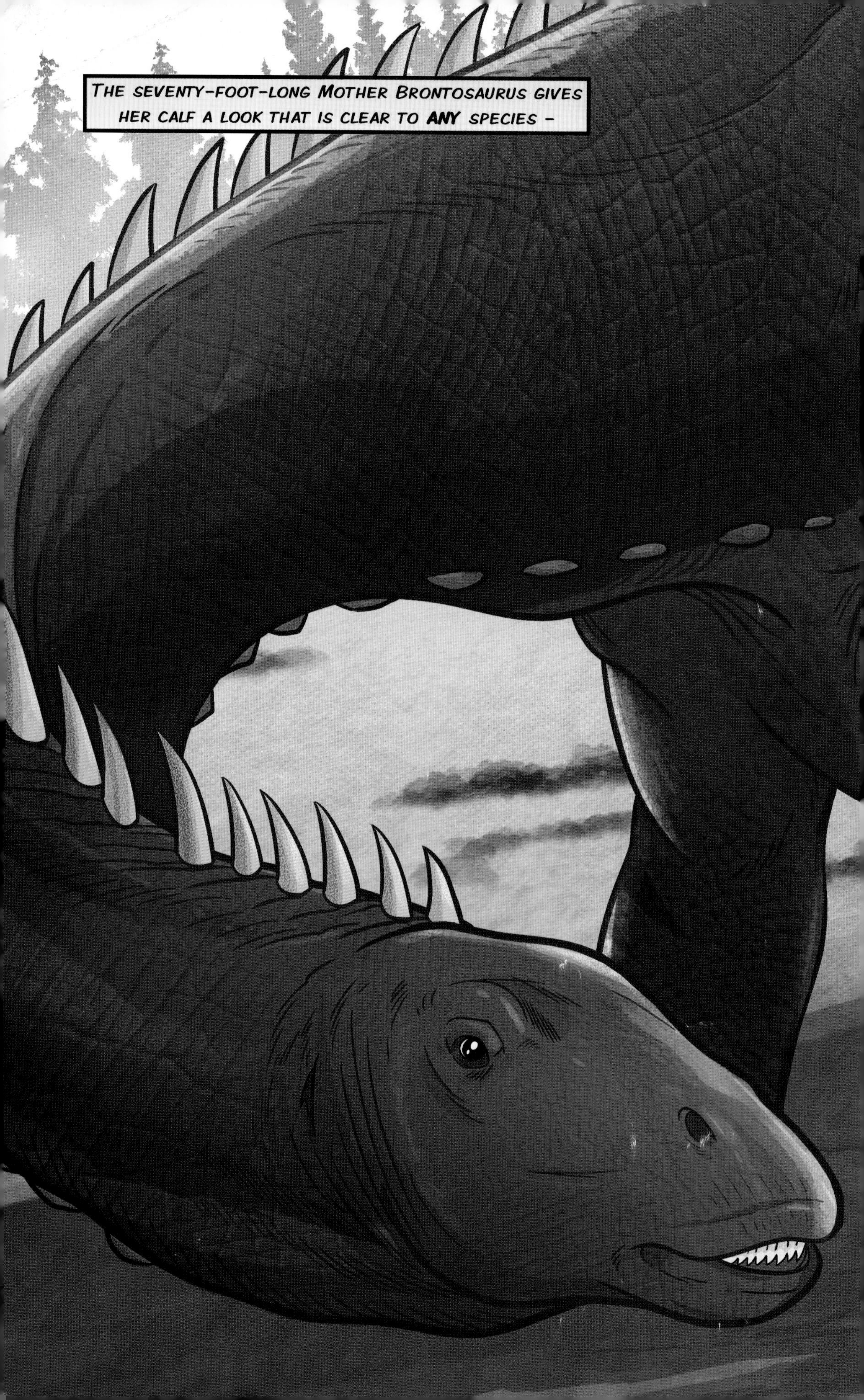
THE SEVENTY-FOOT-LONG MOTHER BRONTOSAURUS GIVES HER CALF A LOOK THAT IS CLEAR TO **ANY** SPECIES -

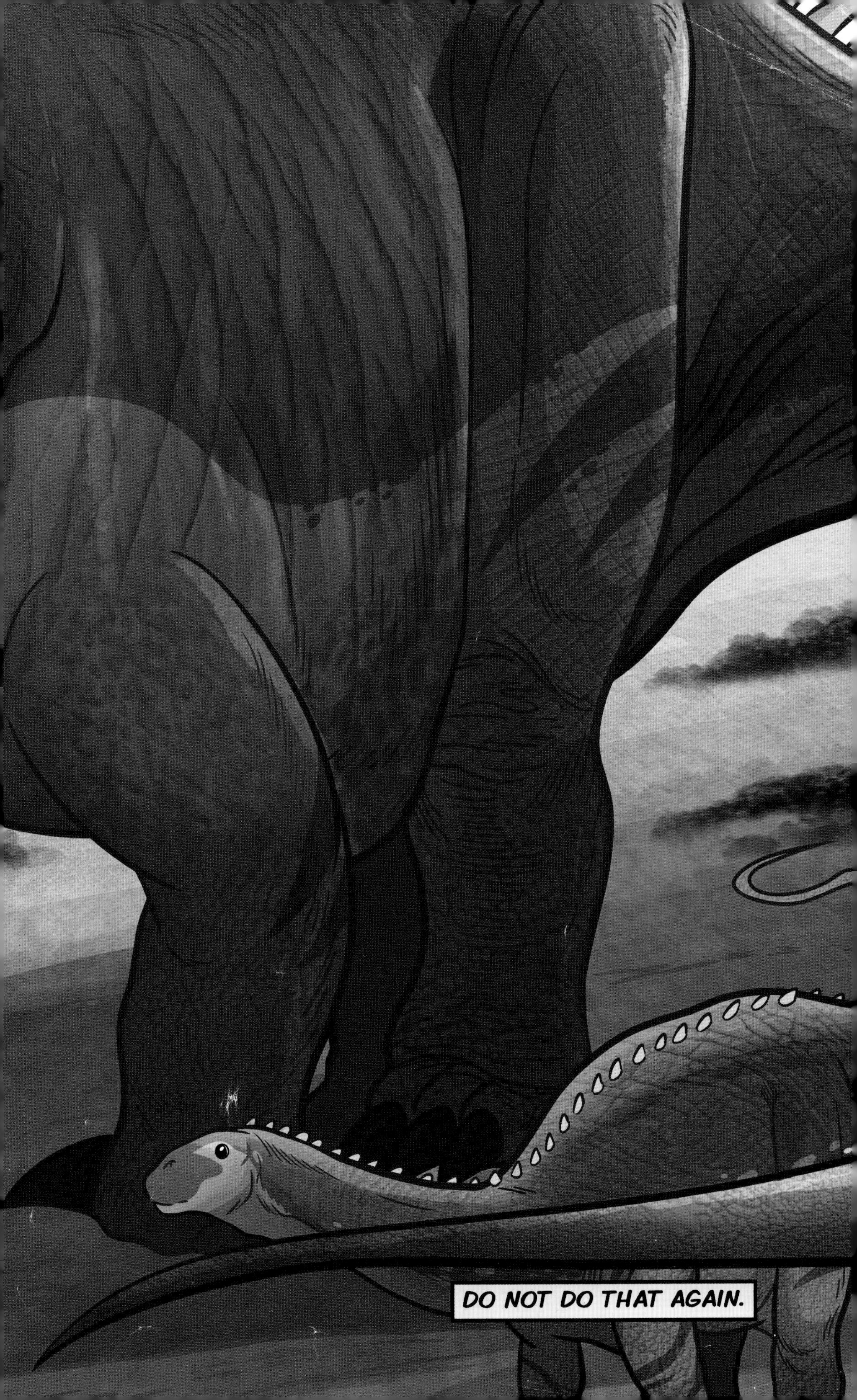
DO NOT DO THAT AGAIN.

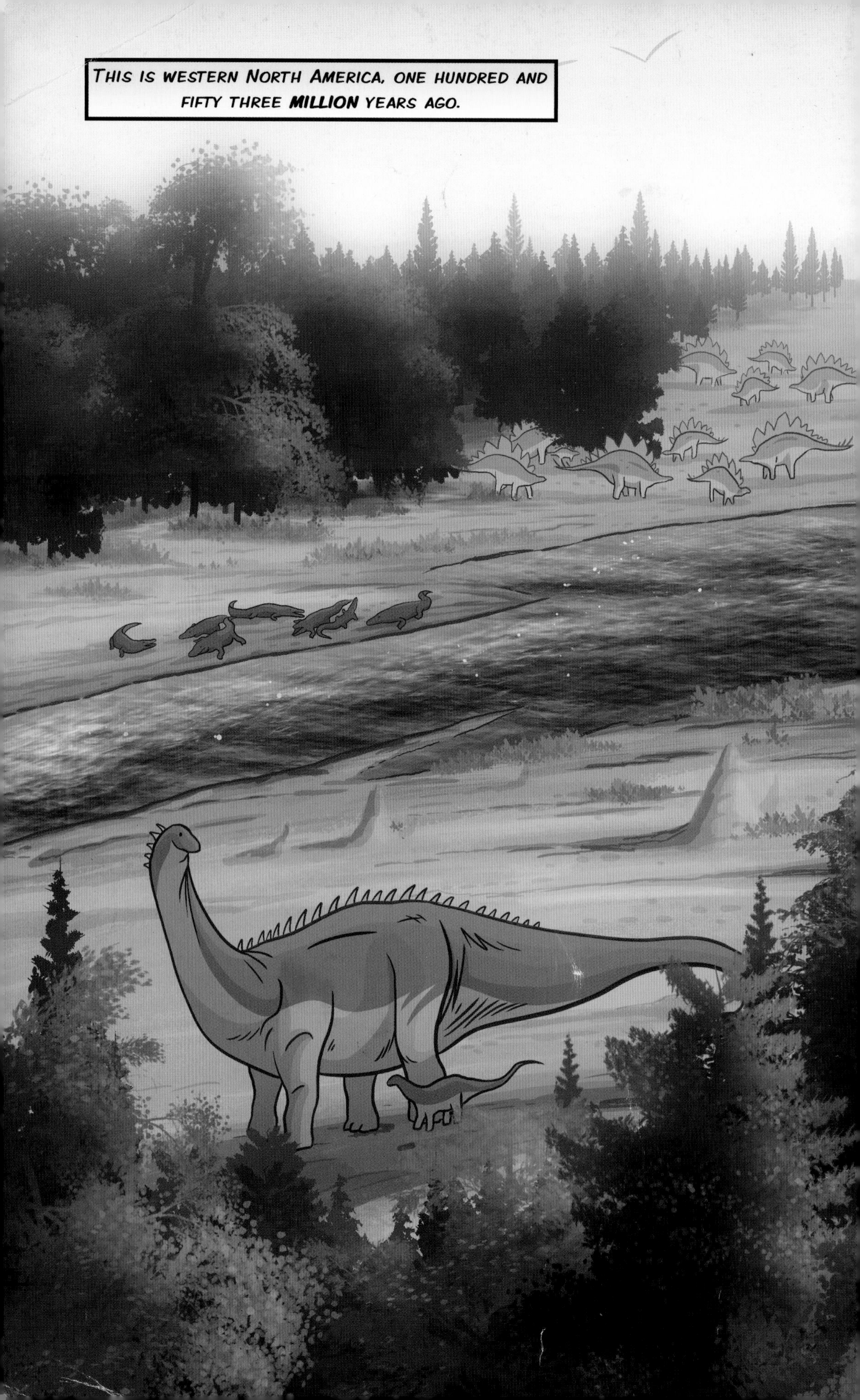
THIS IS WESTERN NORTH AMERICA, ONE HUNDRED AND FIFTY THREE MILLION YEARS AGO.

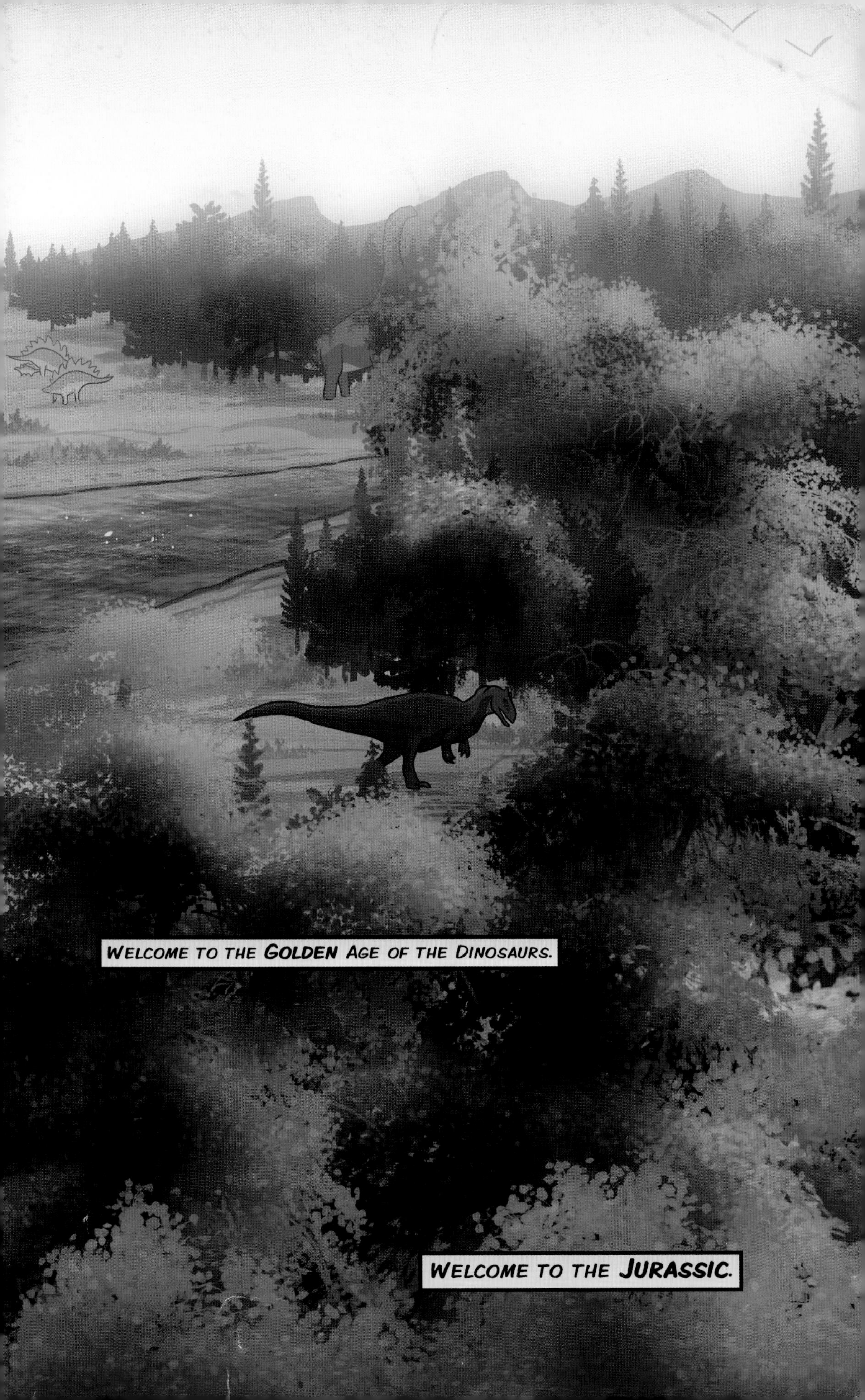
WELCOME TO THE GOLDEN AGE OF THE DINOSAURS.
WELCOME TO THE JURASSIC.

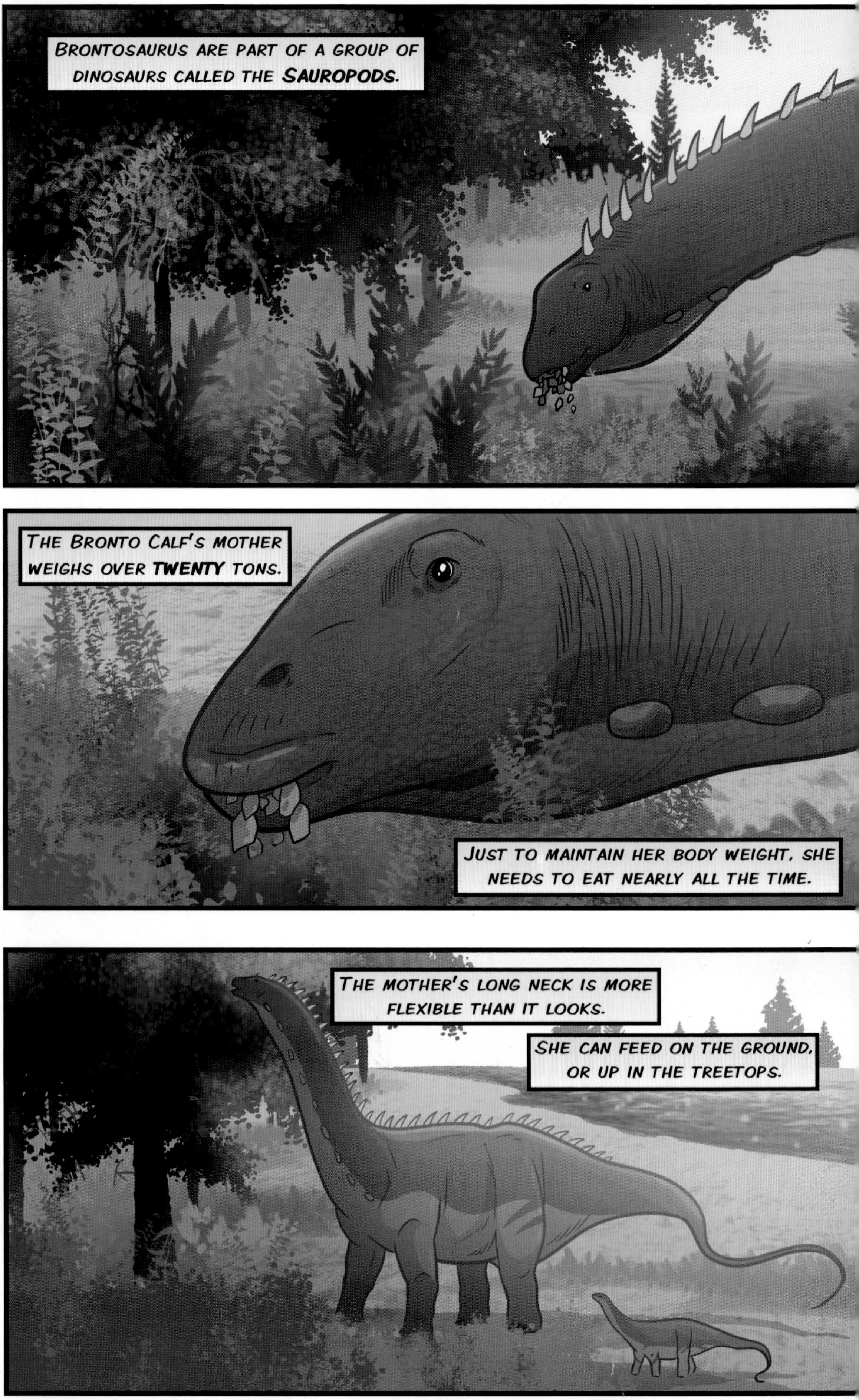
BRONTOSAURUS ARE PART OF A GROUP OF DINOSAURS CALLED THE **SAUROPODS**.
THE BRONTO CALF'S MOTHER WEIGHS OVER **TWENTY** TONS.
JUST TO MAINTAIN HER BODY WEIGHT, SHE NEEDS TO EAT NEARLY ALL THE TIME.
THE MOTHER'S LONG NECK IS MORE FLEXIBLE THAN IT LOOKS.
SHE CAN FEED ON THE GROUND, OR UP IN THE TREETOPS.

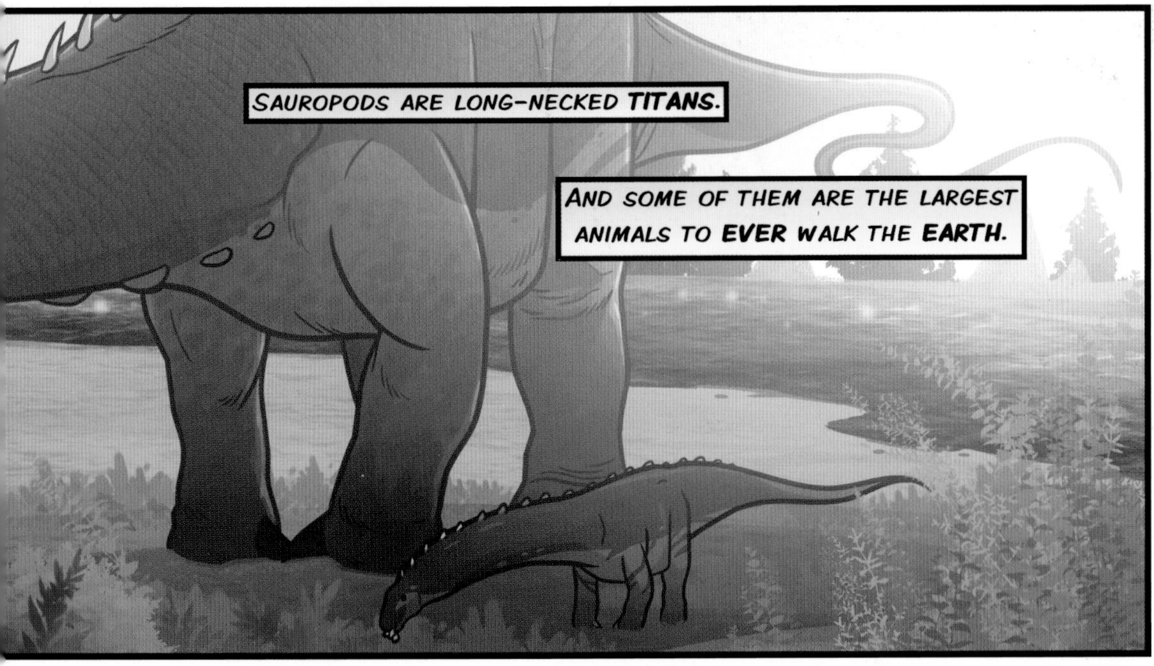
SAUROPODS ARE LONG-NECKED **TITANS.**
AND SOME OF THEM ARE THE LARGEST ANIMALS TO **EVER** WALK THE **EARTH.**

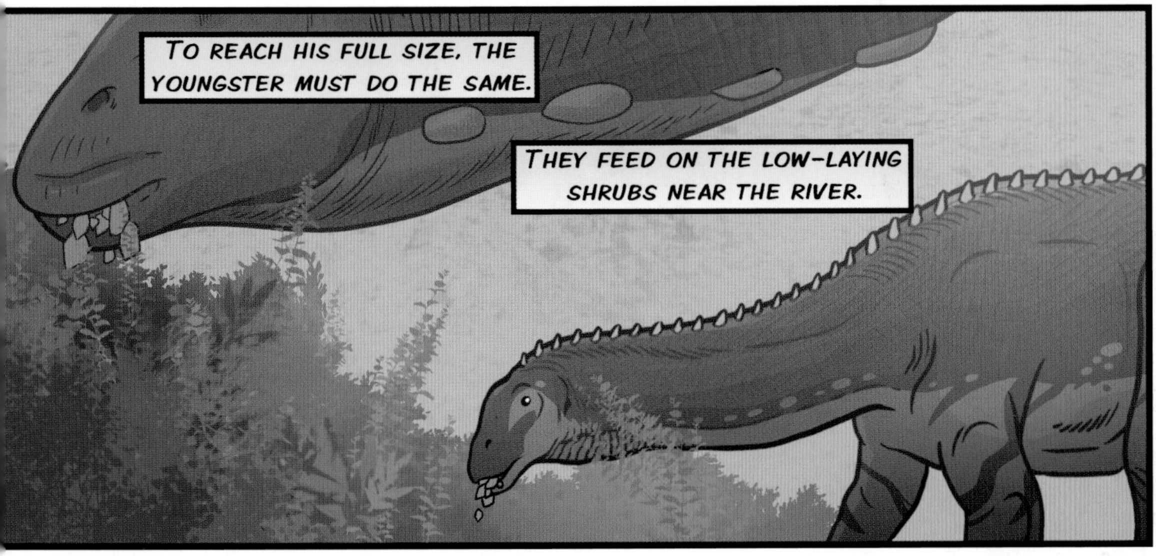
TO REACH HIS FULL SIZE, THE YOUNGSTER MUST DO THE SAME.
THEY FEED ON THE LOW-LAYING SHRUBS NEAR THE RIVER.

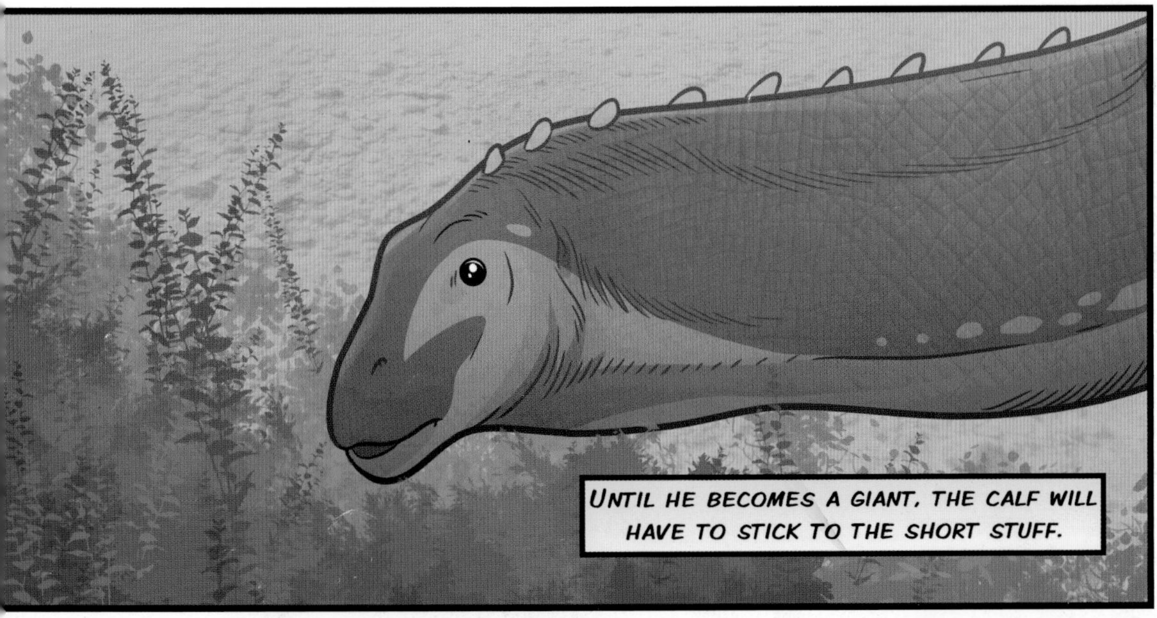
UNTIL HE BECOMES A GIANT, THE CALF WILL HAVE TO STICK TO THE SHORT STUFF.

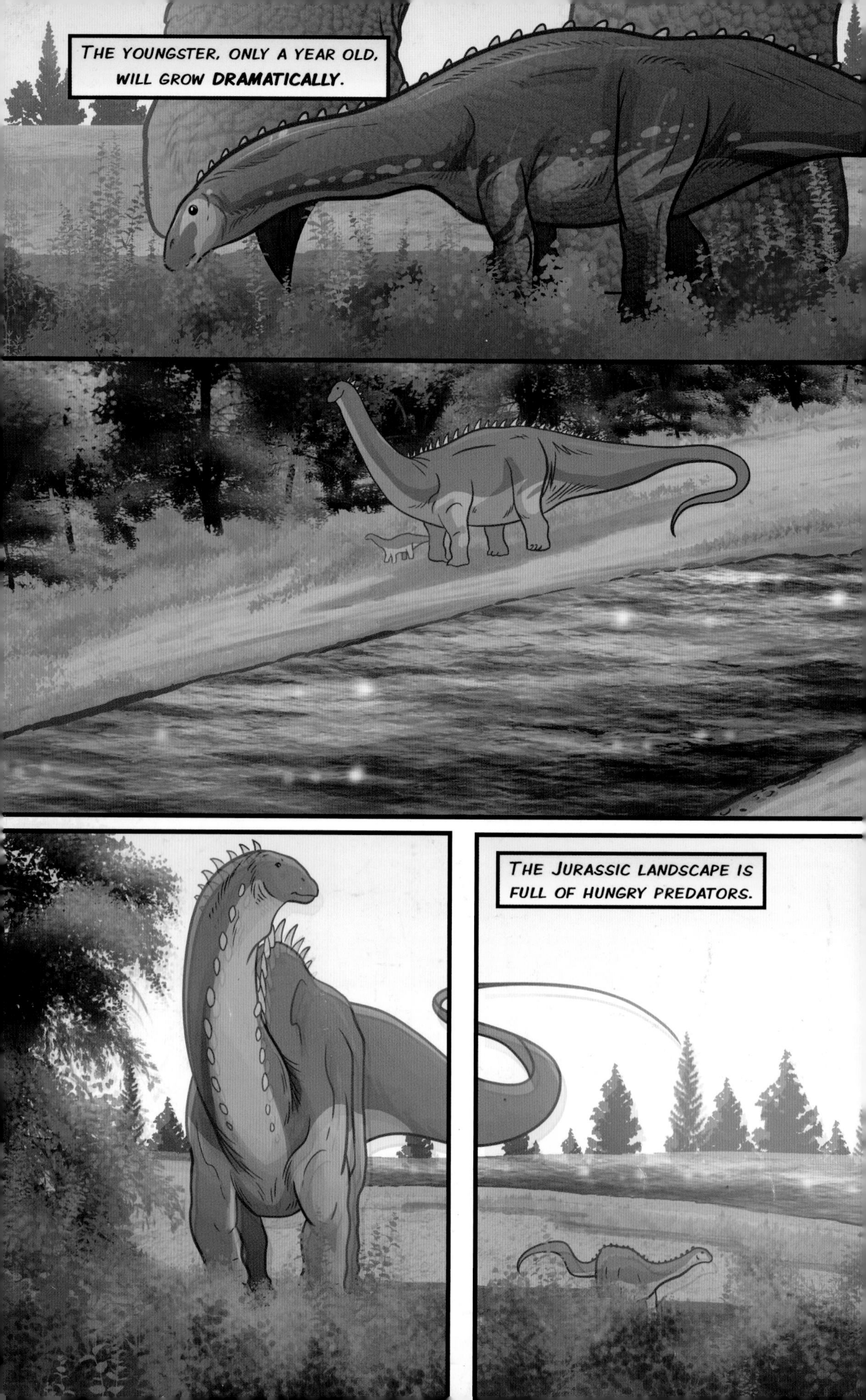
THE YOUNGSTER, ONLY A YEAR OLD, WILL GROW **DRAMATICALLY**.
THE JURASSIC LANDSCAPE IS FULL OF HUNGRY PREDATORS.

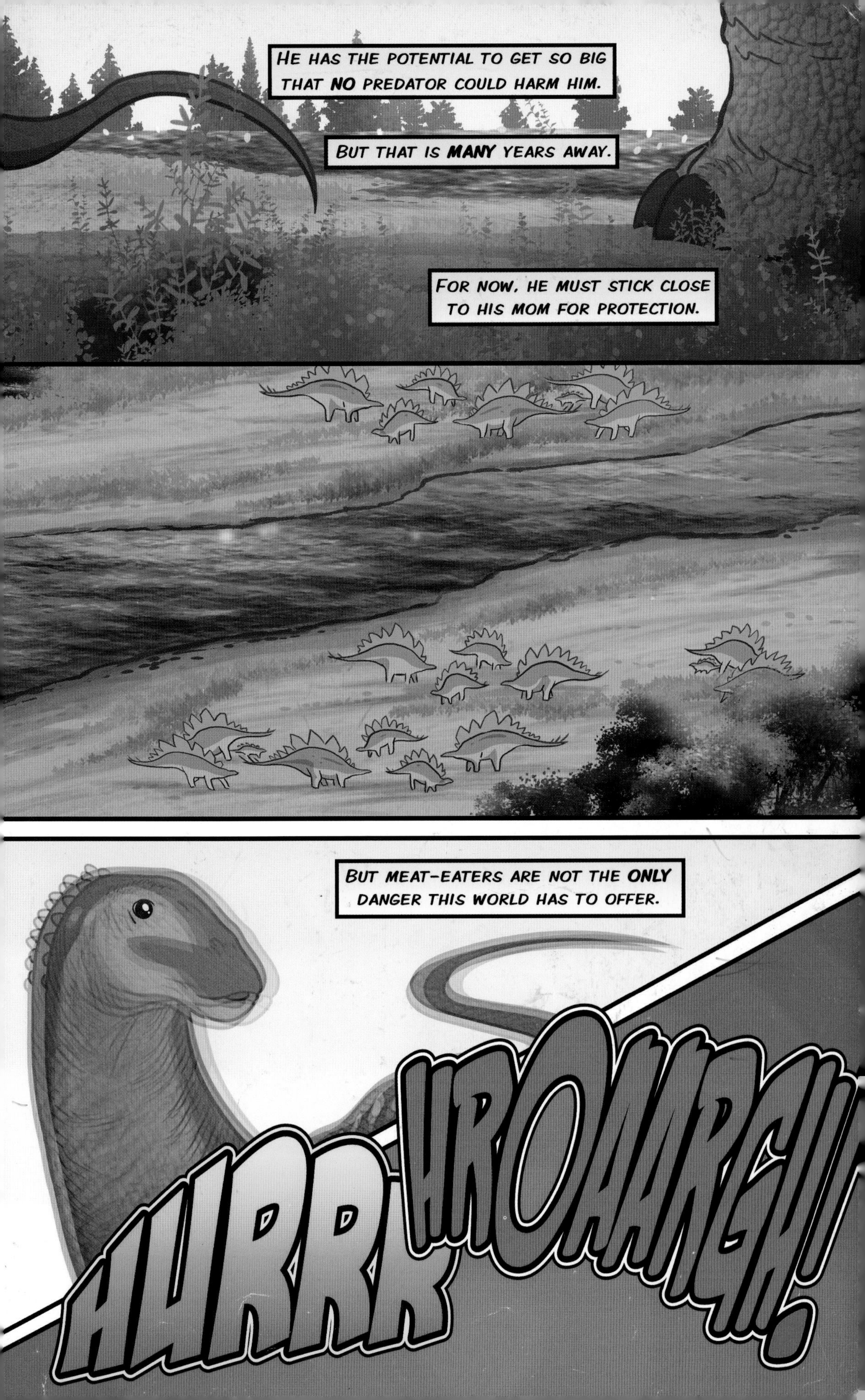
HE HAS THE POTENTIAL TO GET SO BIG THAT NO PREDATOR COULD HARM HIM.
BUT THAT IS MANY YEARS AWAY.
FOR NOW, HE MUST STICK CLOSE TO HIS MOM FOR PROTECTION.
BUT MEAT-EATERS ARE NOT THE ONLY DANGER THIS WORLD HAS TO OFFER.
HURRR
HROAARGH!

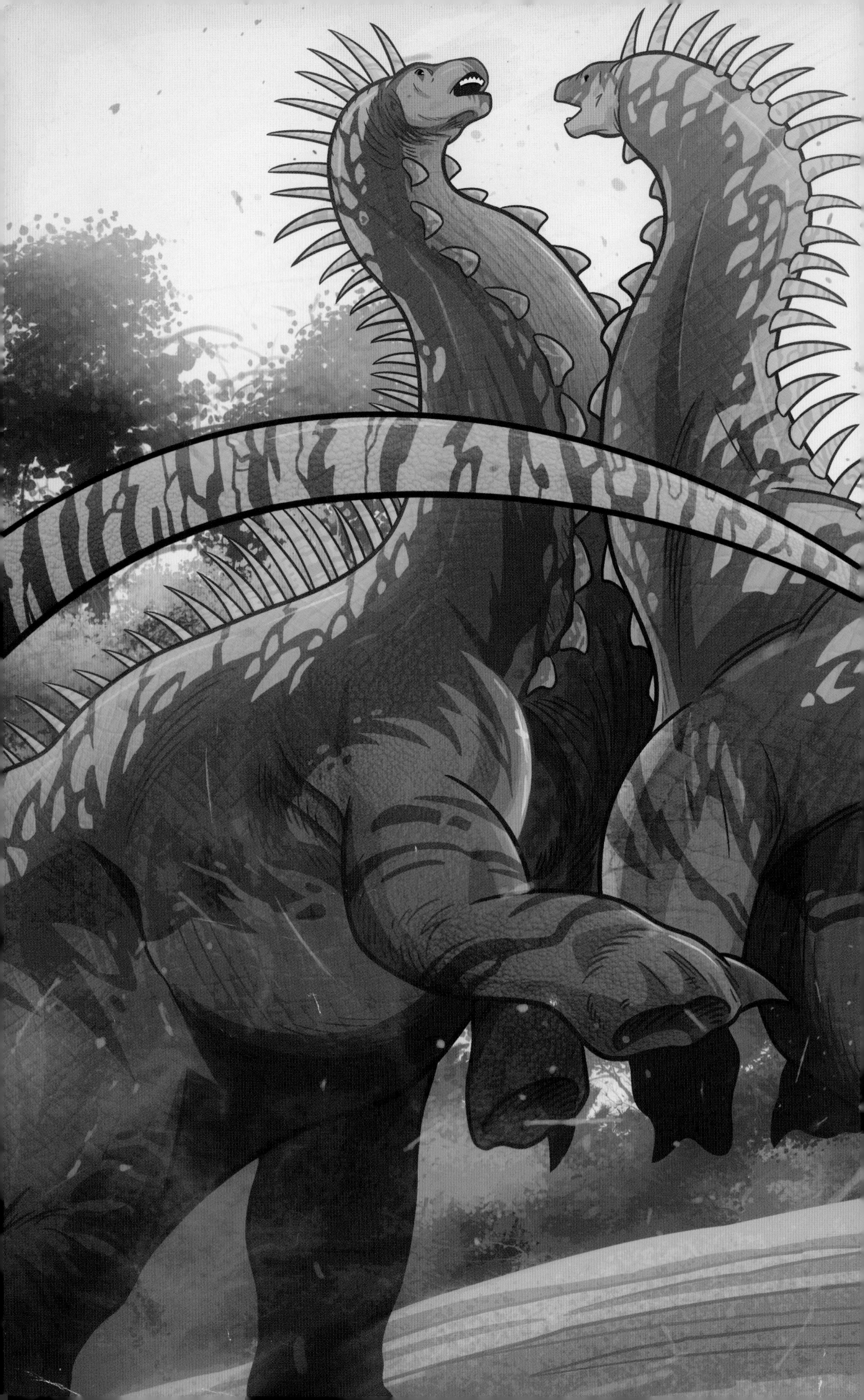

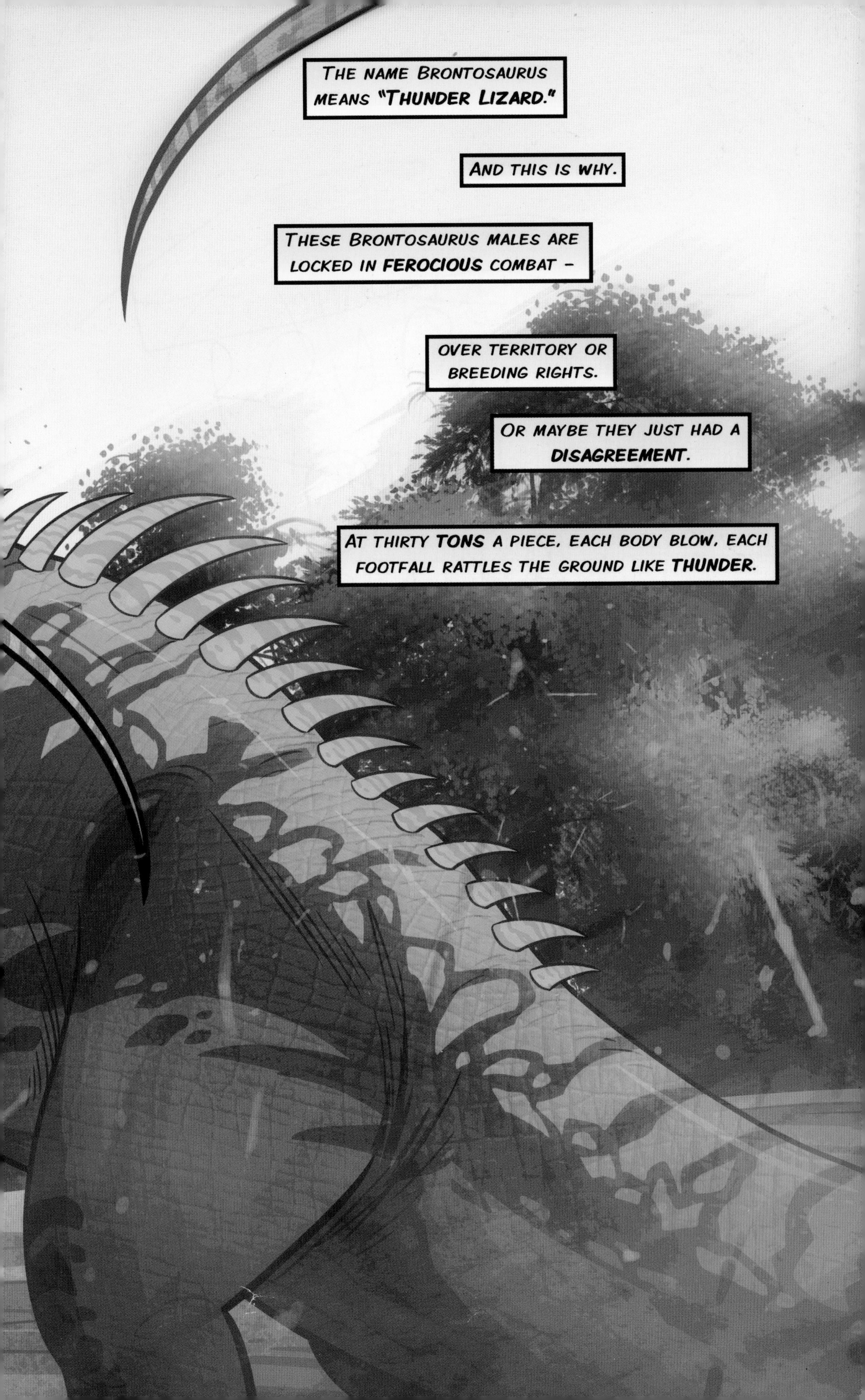
THE NAME BRONTOSAURUS MEANS "THUNDER LIZARD."
AND THIS IS WHY.
THESE BRONTOSAURUS MALES ARE LOCKED IN FEROCIOUS COMBAT –
OVER TERRITORY OR BREEDING RIGHTS.
OR MAYBE THEY JUST HAD A DISAGREEMENT.
AT THIRTY TONS A PIECE, EACH BODY BLOW, EACH FOOTFALL RATTLES THE GROUND LIKE THUNDER.

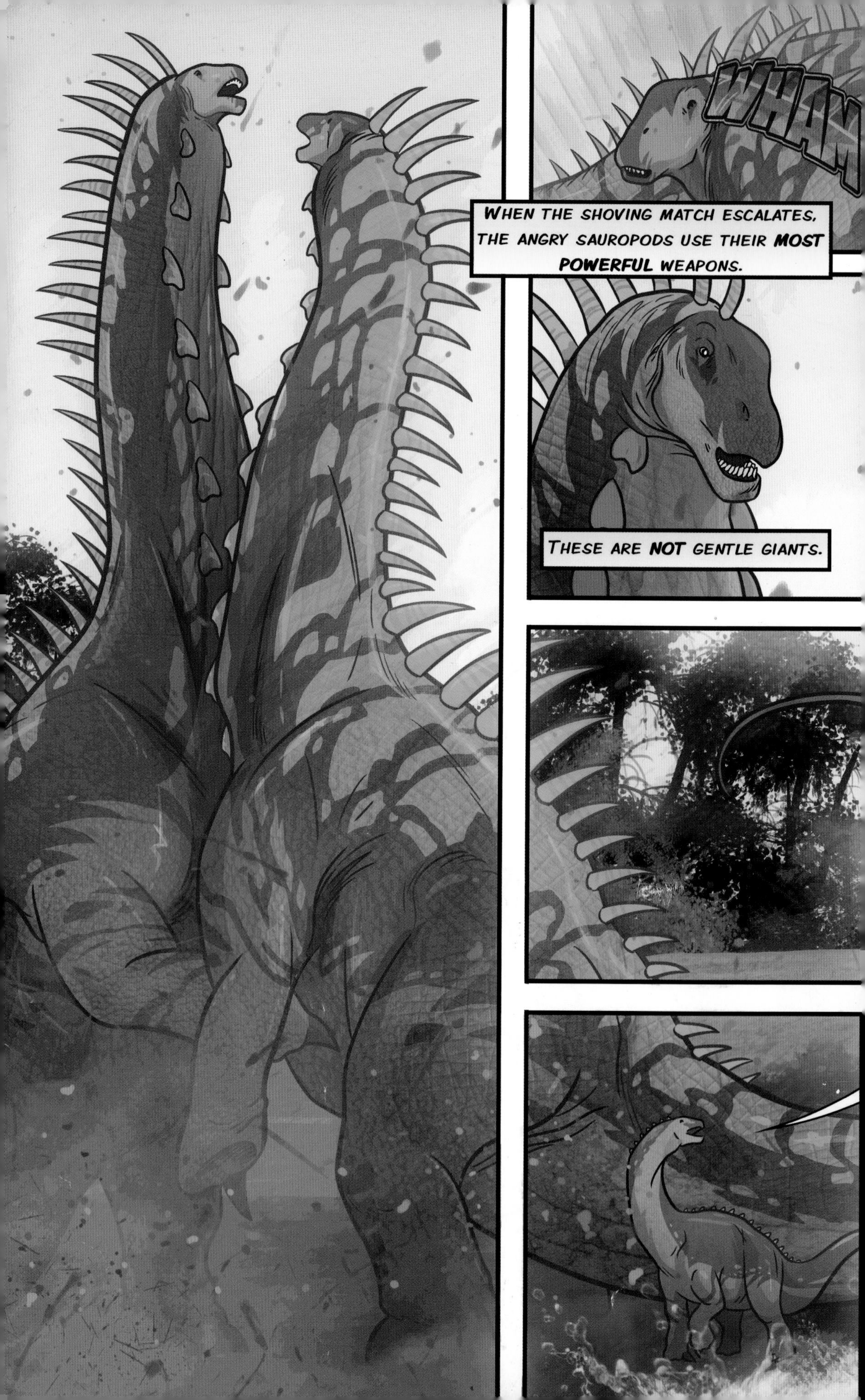
WHAM
WHEN THE SHOVING MATCH ESCALATES, THE ANGRY SAUROPODS USE THEIR MOST POWERFUL WEAPONS.
THESE ARE NOT GENTLE GIANTS.

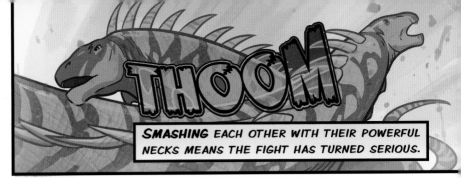

SMASHING EACH OTHER WITH THEIR POWERFUL NECKS MEANS THE FIGHT HAS TURNED SERIOUS.

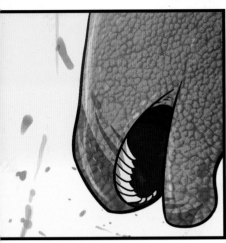

RHUR!

GAAAH!

IN THE CHAOS, IT'S EASY TO GET CAUGHT IN THE CROSSFIRE.

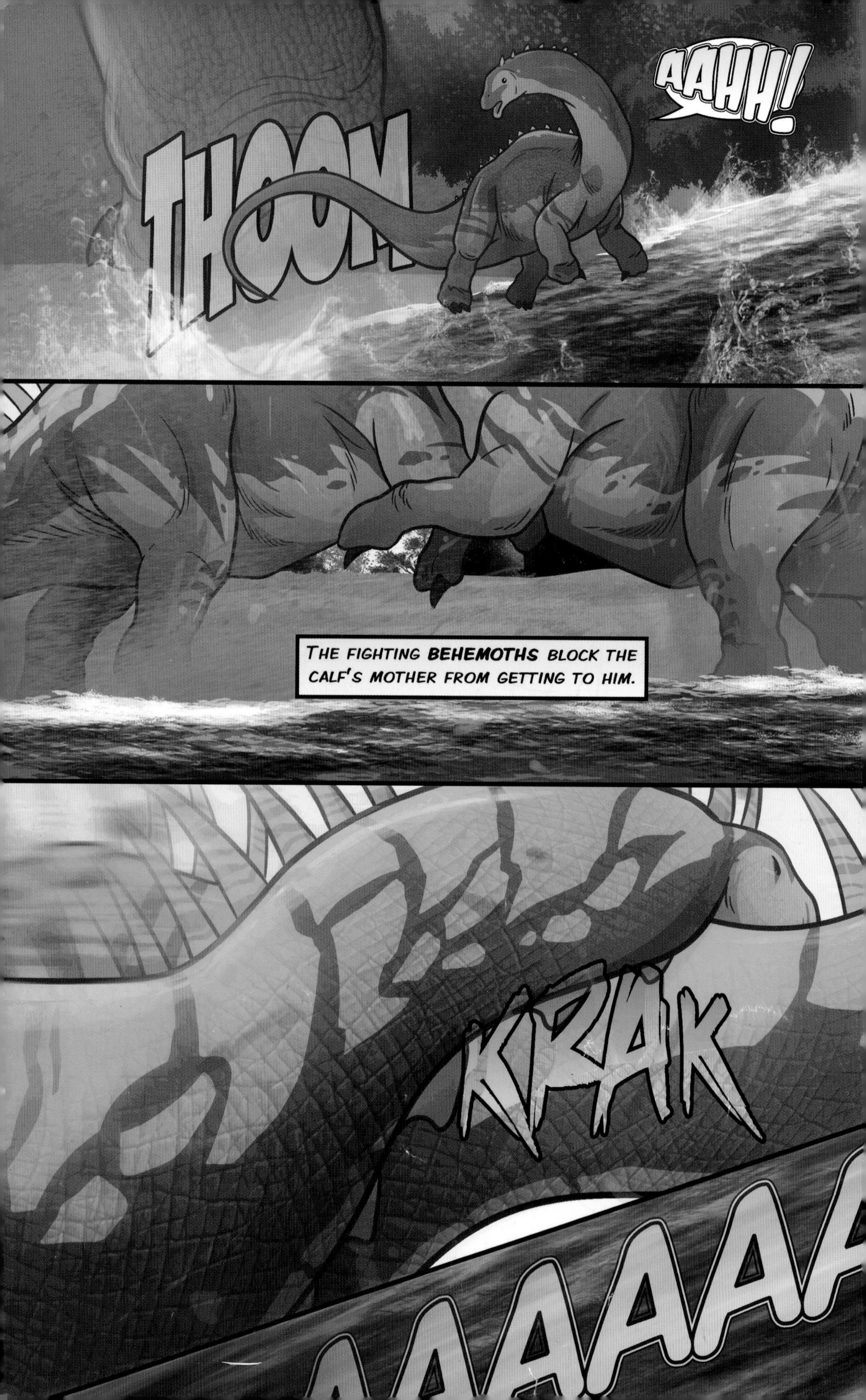
THOOM
AAHH!
THE FIGHTING **BEHEMOTHS** BLOCK THE CALF'S MOTHER FROM GETTING TO HIM.
KRAK
AAAAA

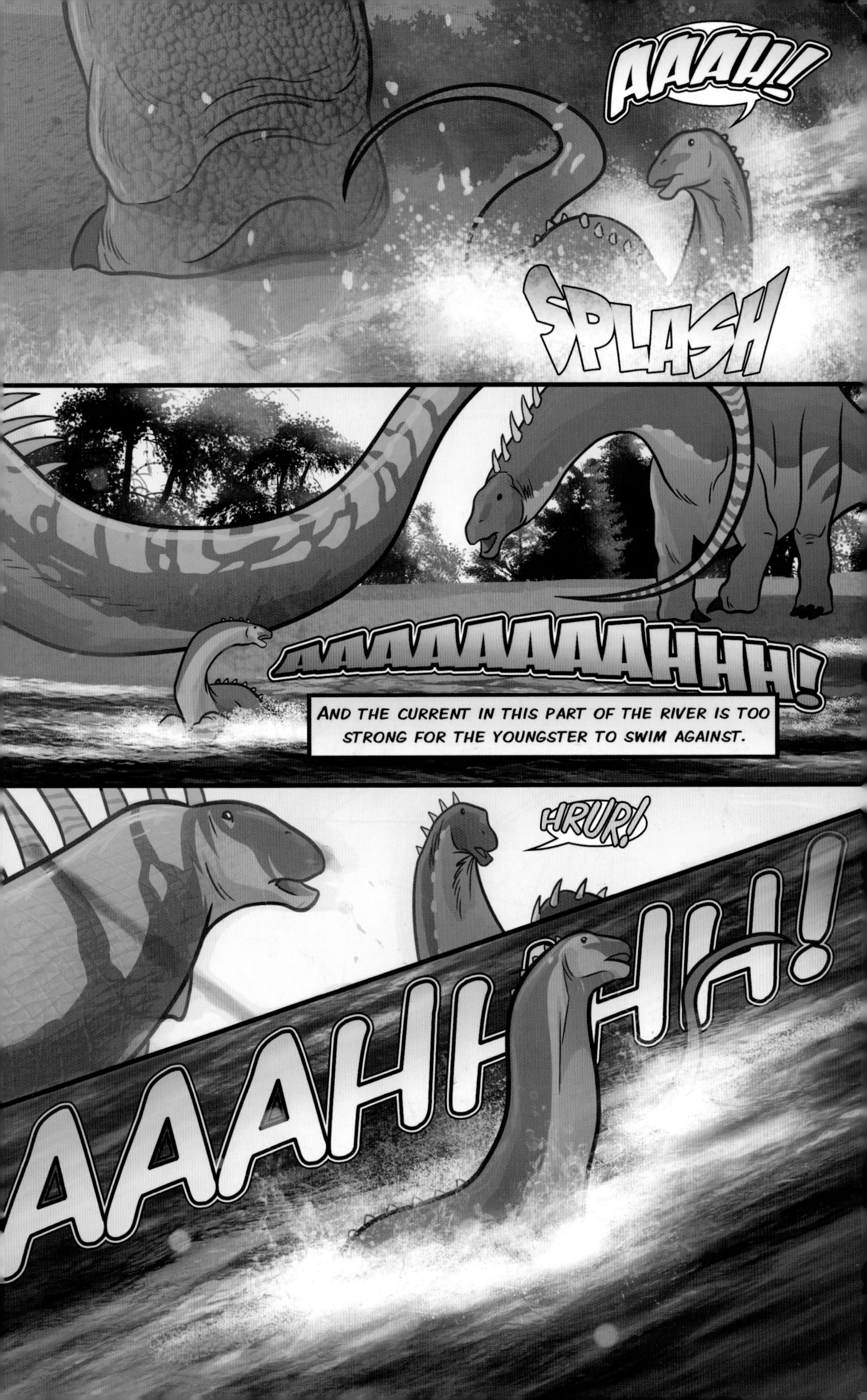
AAAH!!
SPLASH
AAAAAAAAAAHHH!
AND THE CURRENT IN THIS PART OF THE RIVER IS TOO STRONG FOR THE YOUNGSTER TO SWIM AGAINST.
HRUR!
AAAHHHHHH!

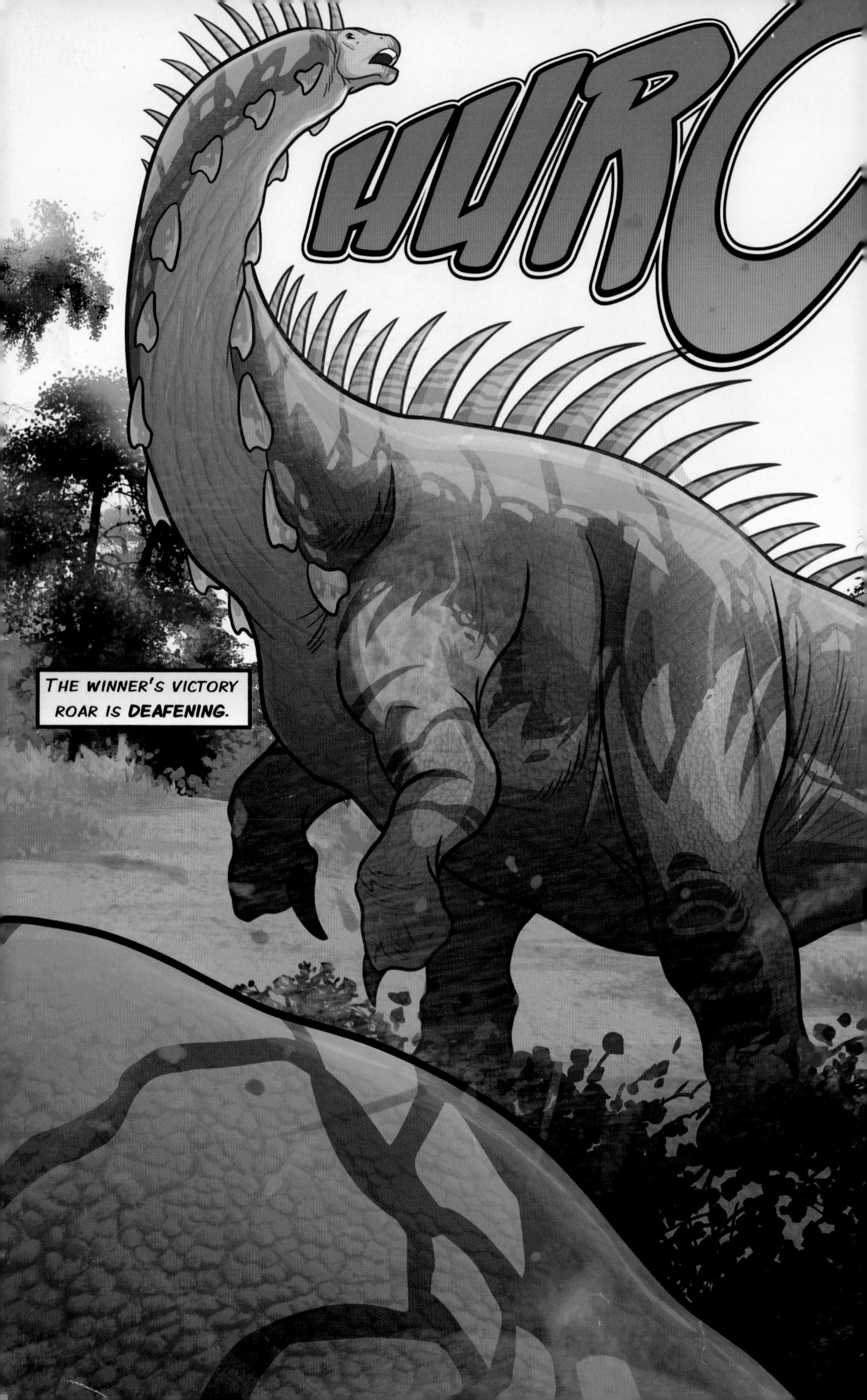
HURC
THE WINNER'S VICTORY ROAR IS **DEAFENING.**

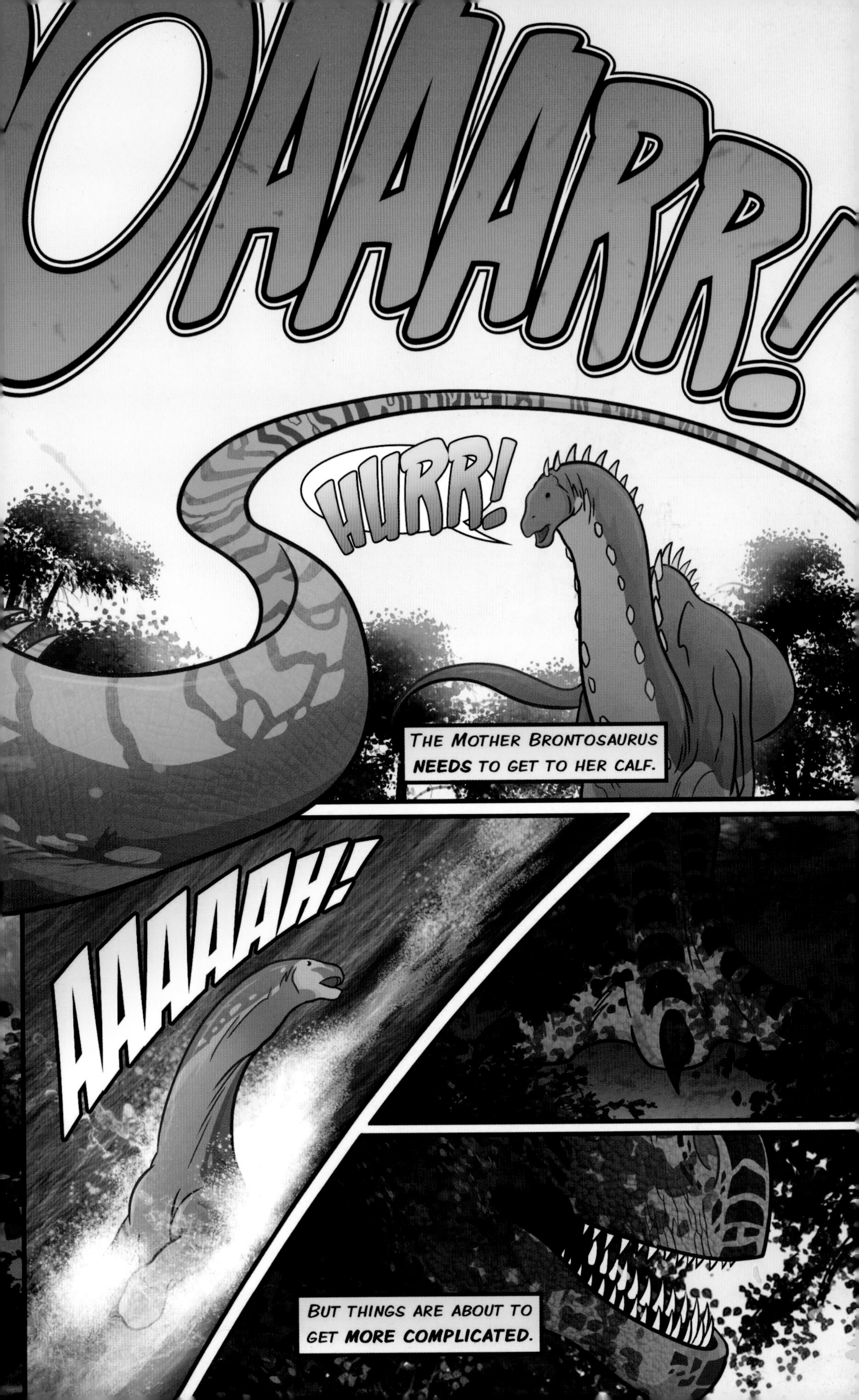
RAAARRR!
HURR!
THE MOTHER BRONTOSAURUS NEEDS TO GET TO HER CALF.
AAAAAH!
BUT THINGS ARE ABOUT TO GET MORE COMPLICATED.

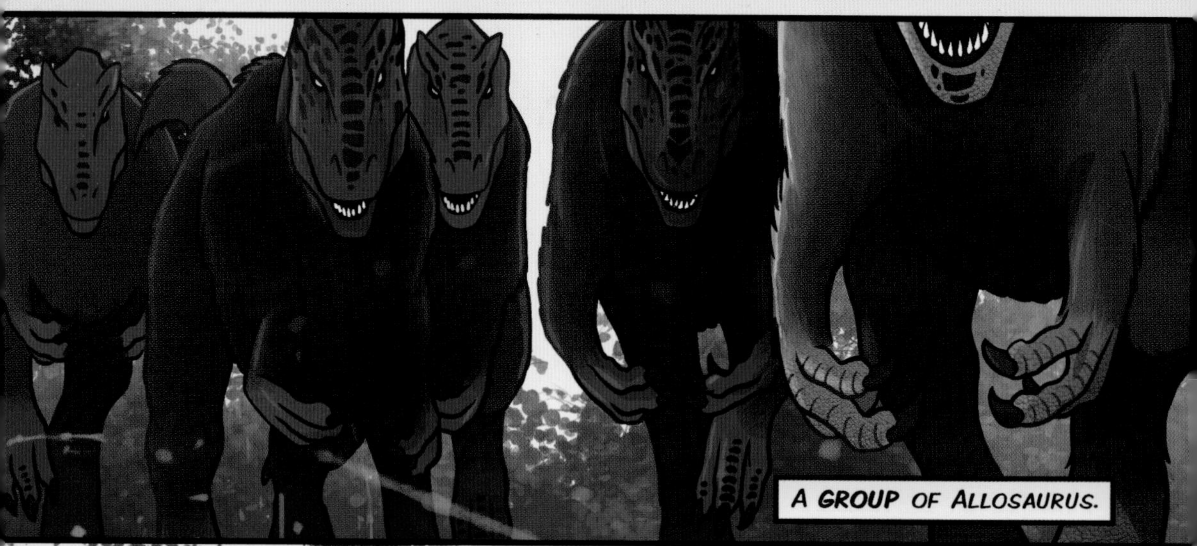
A GROUP OF ALLOSAURUS.

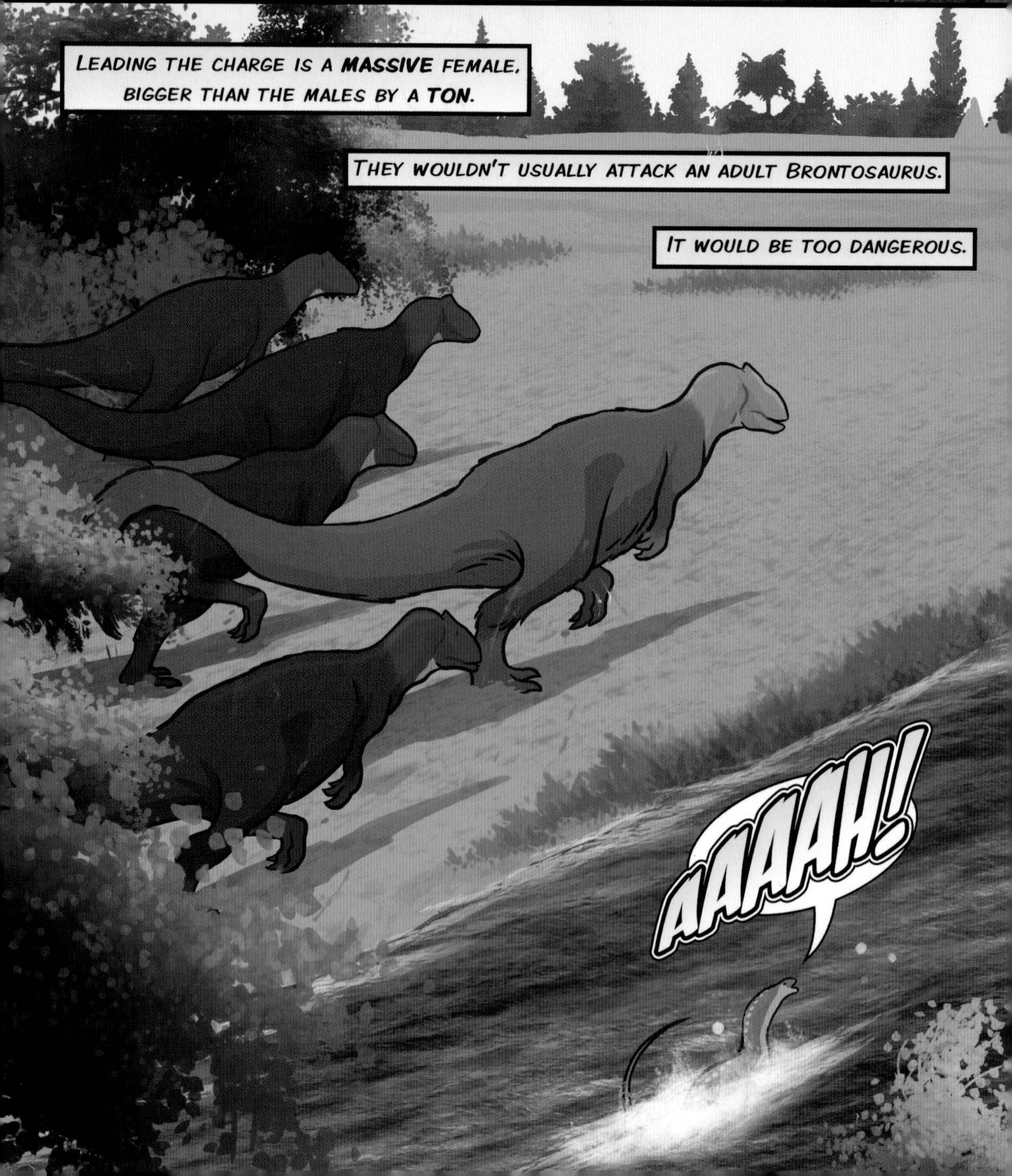
LEADING THE CHARGE IS A MASSIVE FEMALE, BIGGER THAN THE MALES BY A TON.
THEY WOULDN'T USUALLY ATTACK AN ADULT BRONTOSAURUS.
IT WOULD BE TOO DANGEROUS.
AAAAH!

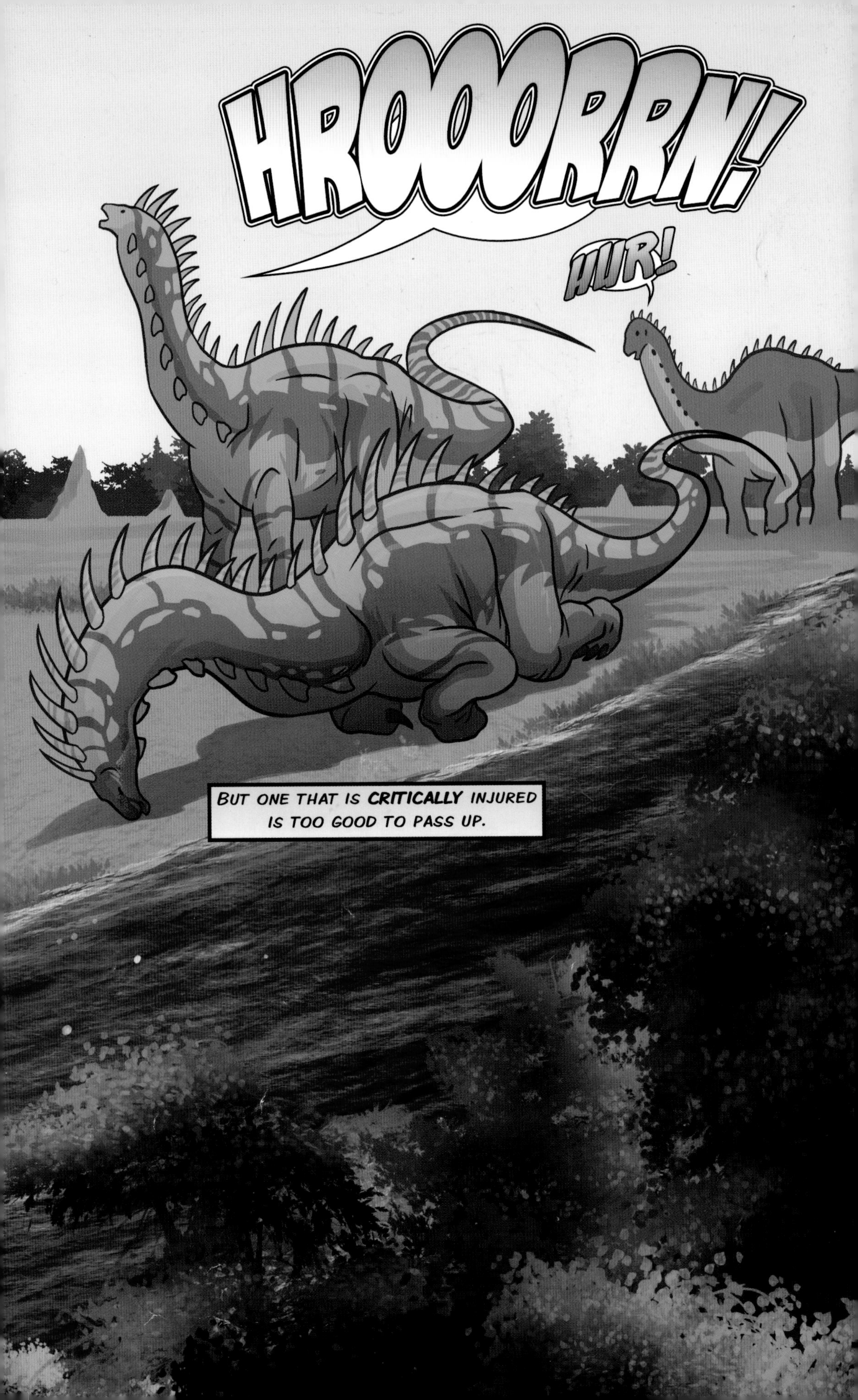
HROOORRRN!
HUR!
BUT ONE THAT IS **CRITICALLY** INJURED IS TOO GOOD TO PASS UP.

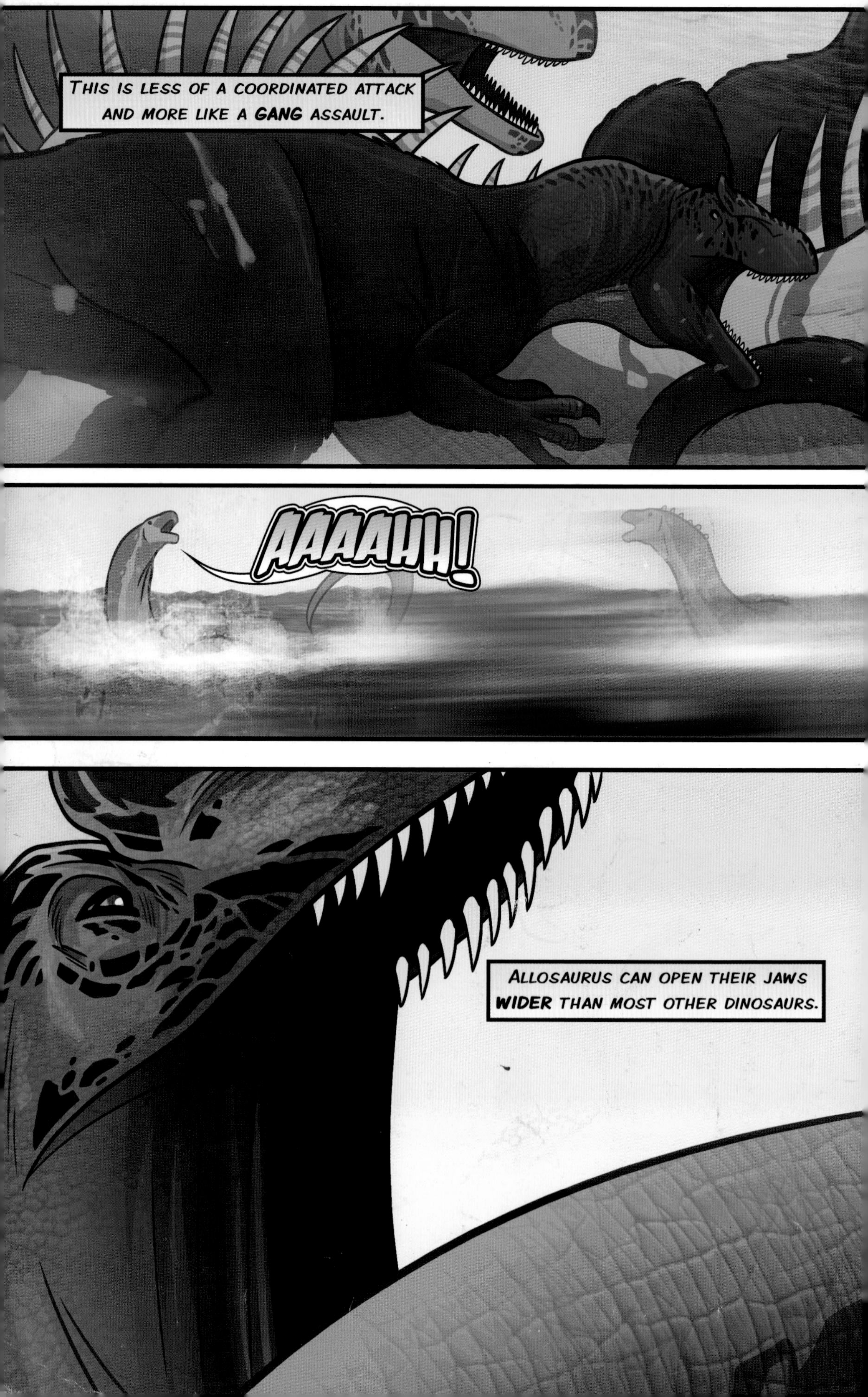
THIS IS LESS OF A COORDINATED ATTACK AND MORE LIKE A GANG ASSAULT.
AAAAHH!
ALLOSAURUS CAN OPEN THEIR JAWS WIDER THAN MOST OTHER DINOSAURS.

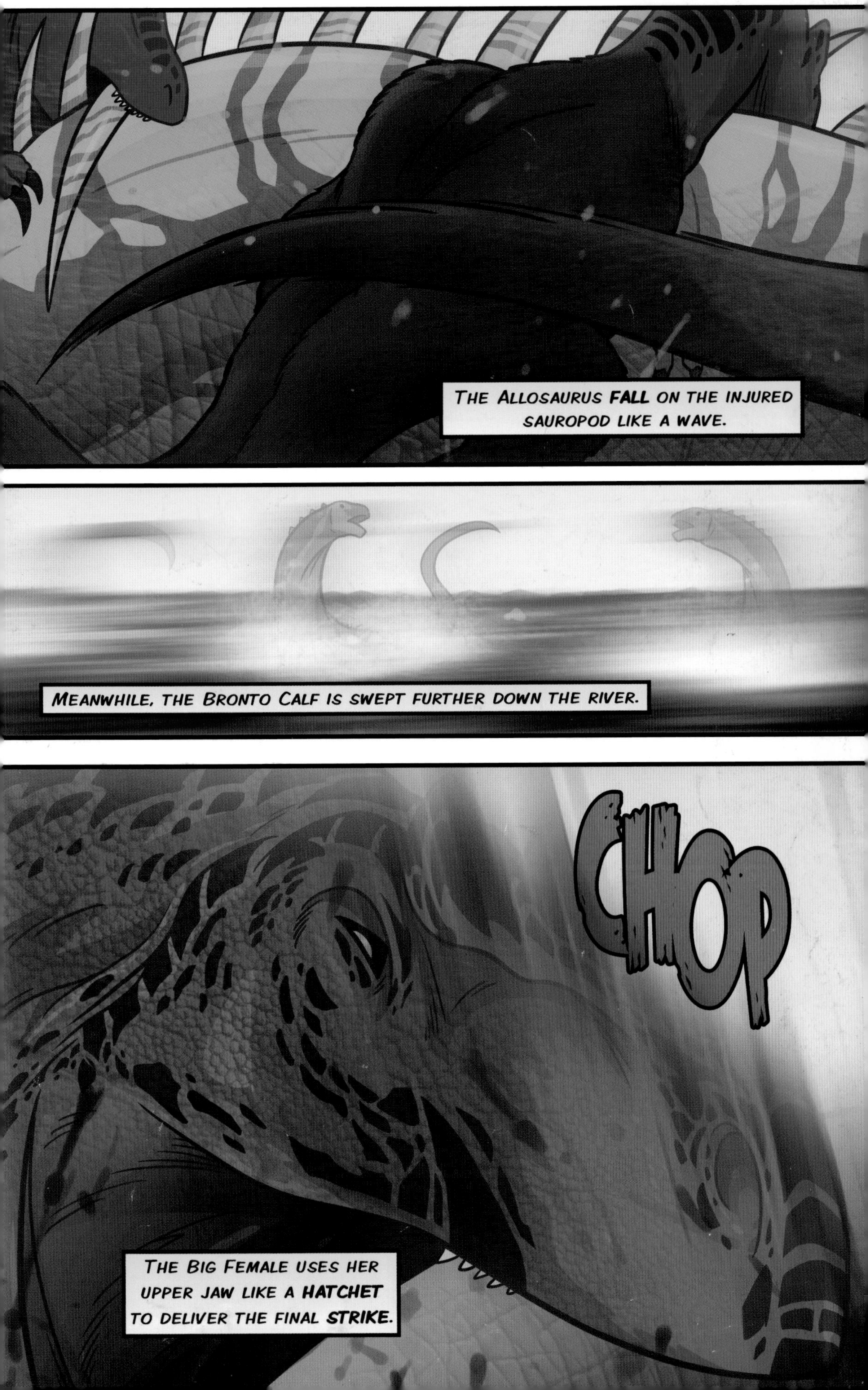
The Allosaurus FALL on the injured sauropod like a wave.
Meanwhile, the Bronto Calf is swept further down the river.
CHOP
The Big Female uses her upper jaw like a HATCHET to deliver the final STRIKE.

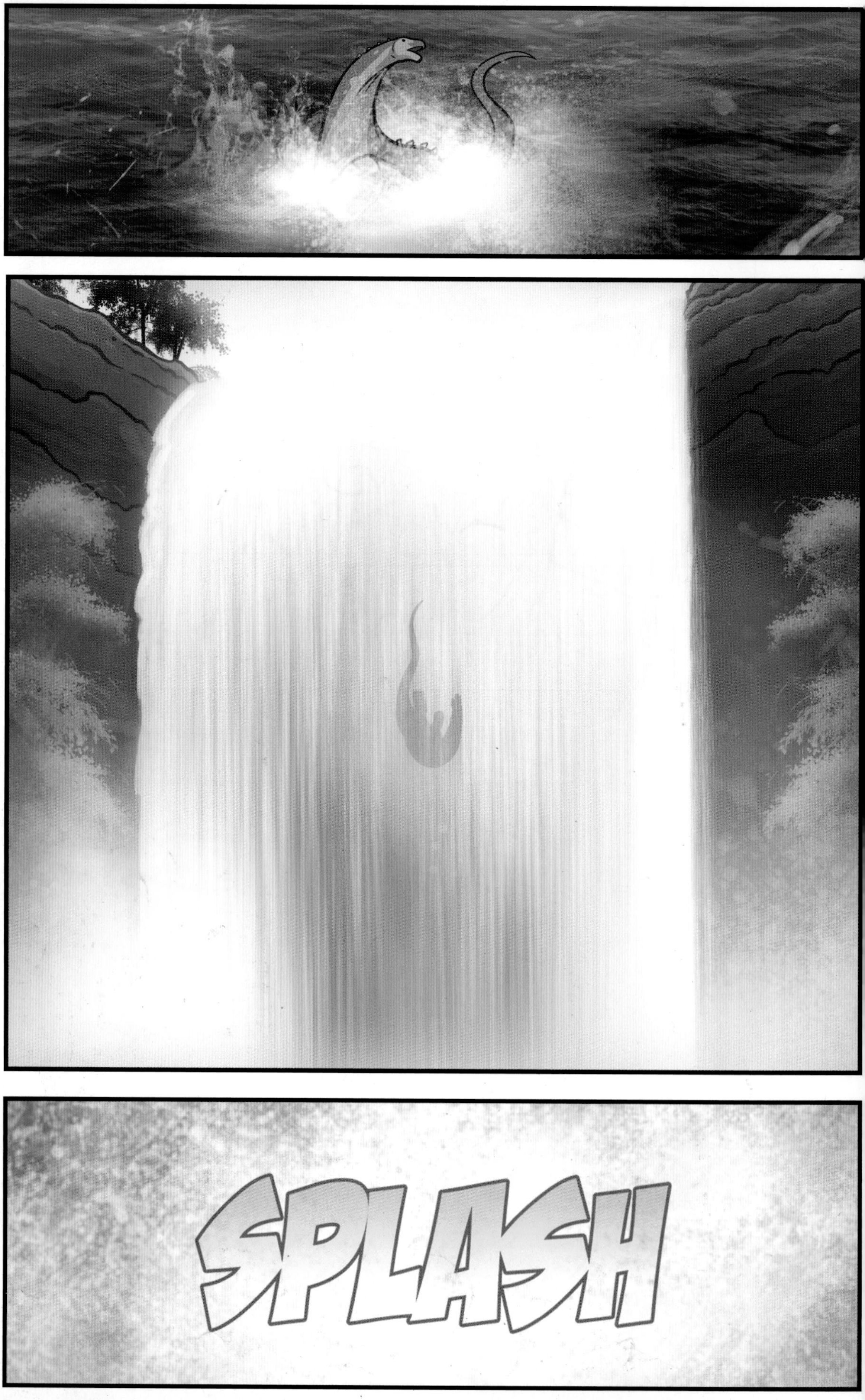
SPLASH

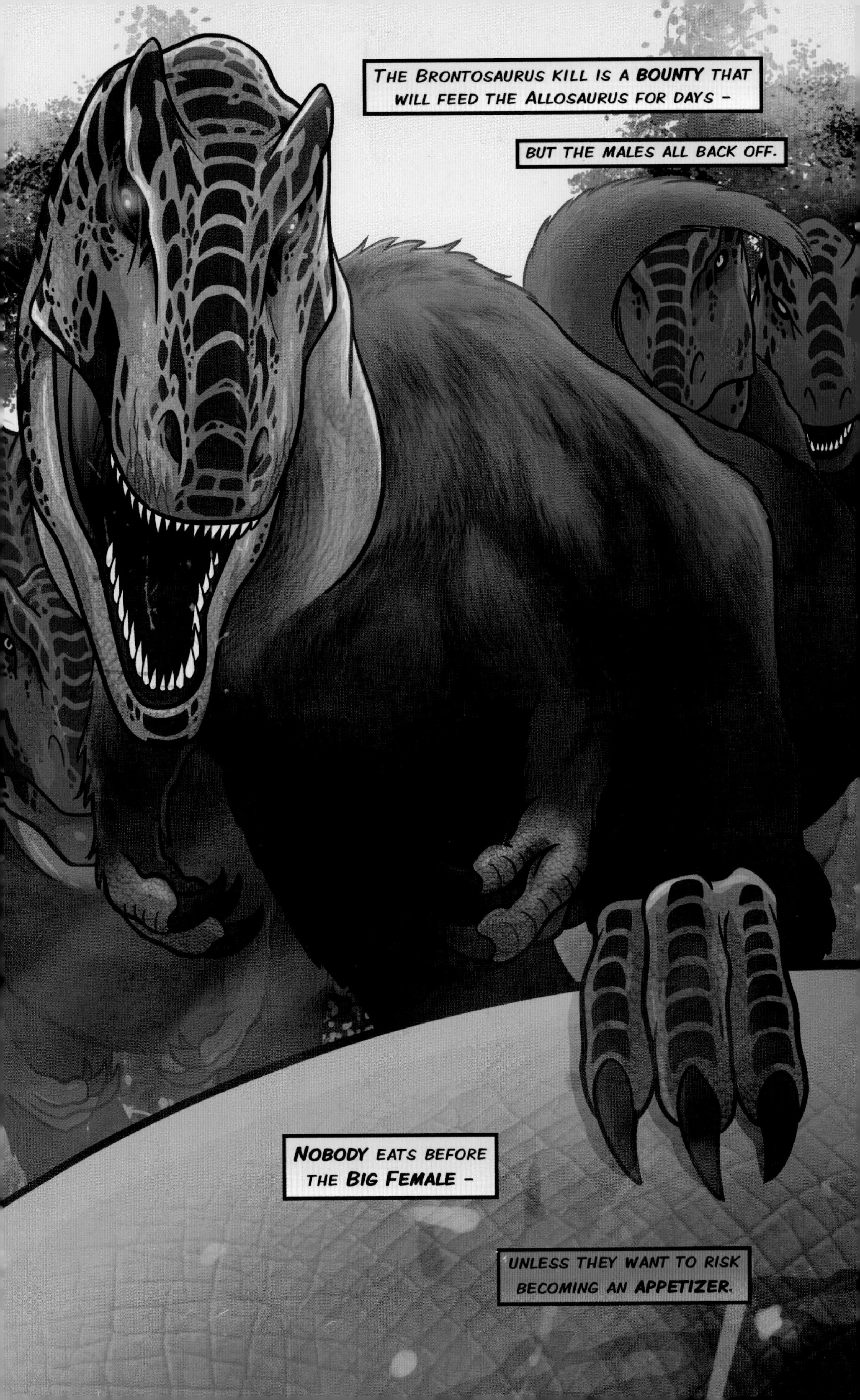
THE BRONTOSAURUS KILL IS A BOUNTY THAT WILL FEED THE ALLOSAURUS FOR DAYS -
BUT THE MALES ALL BACK OFF.
NOBODY EATS BEFORE THE BIG FEMALE -
UNLESS THEY WANT TO RISK BECOMING AN APPETIZER.

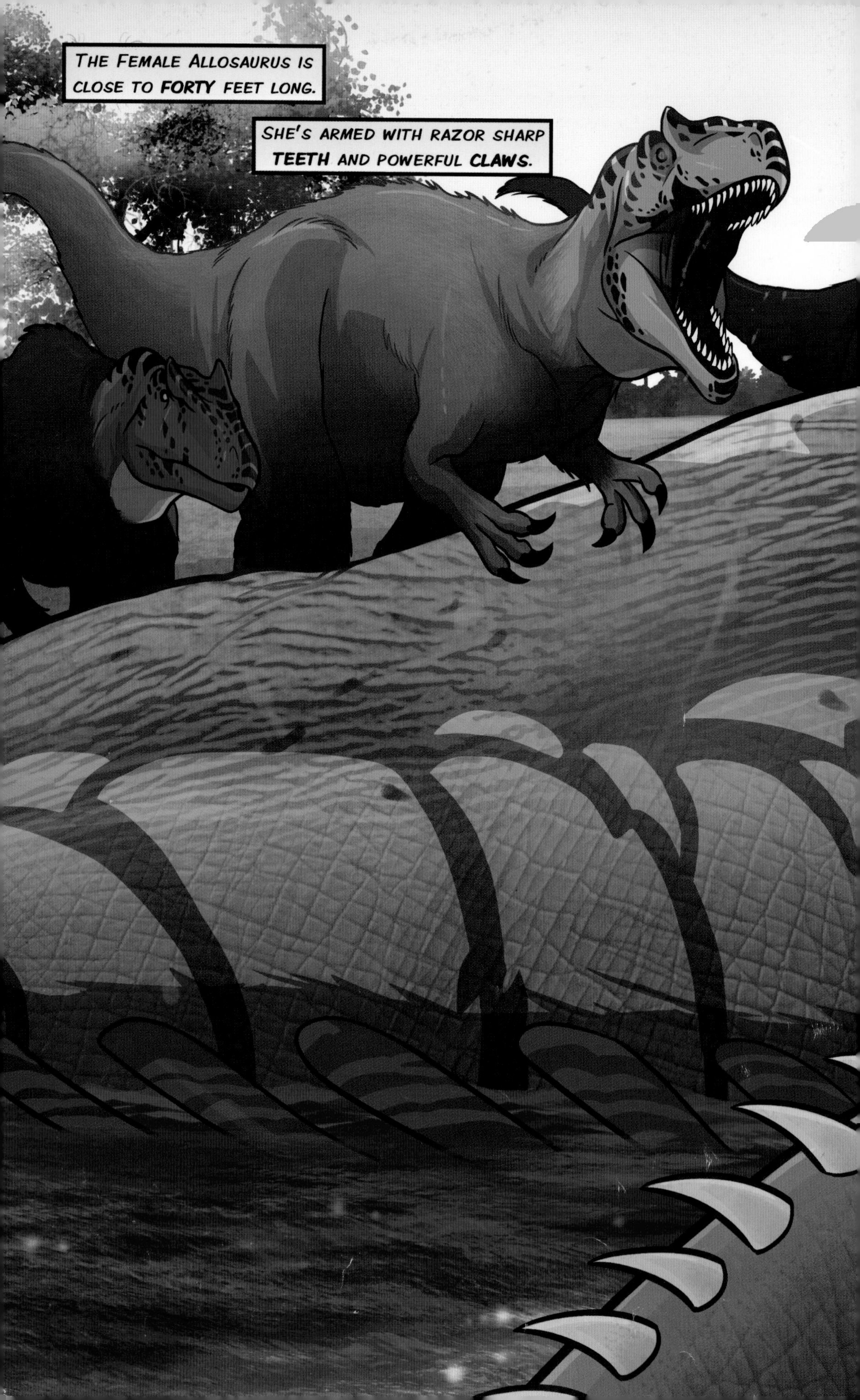
THE FEMALE ALLOSAURUS IS CLOSE TO **FORTY** FEET LONG.
SHE'S ARMED WITH RAZOR SHARP **TEETH** AND POWERFUL **CLAWS**.

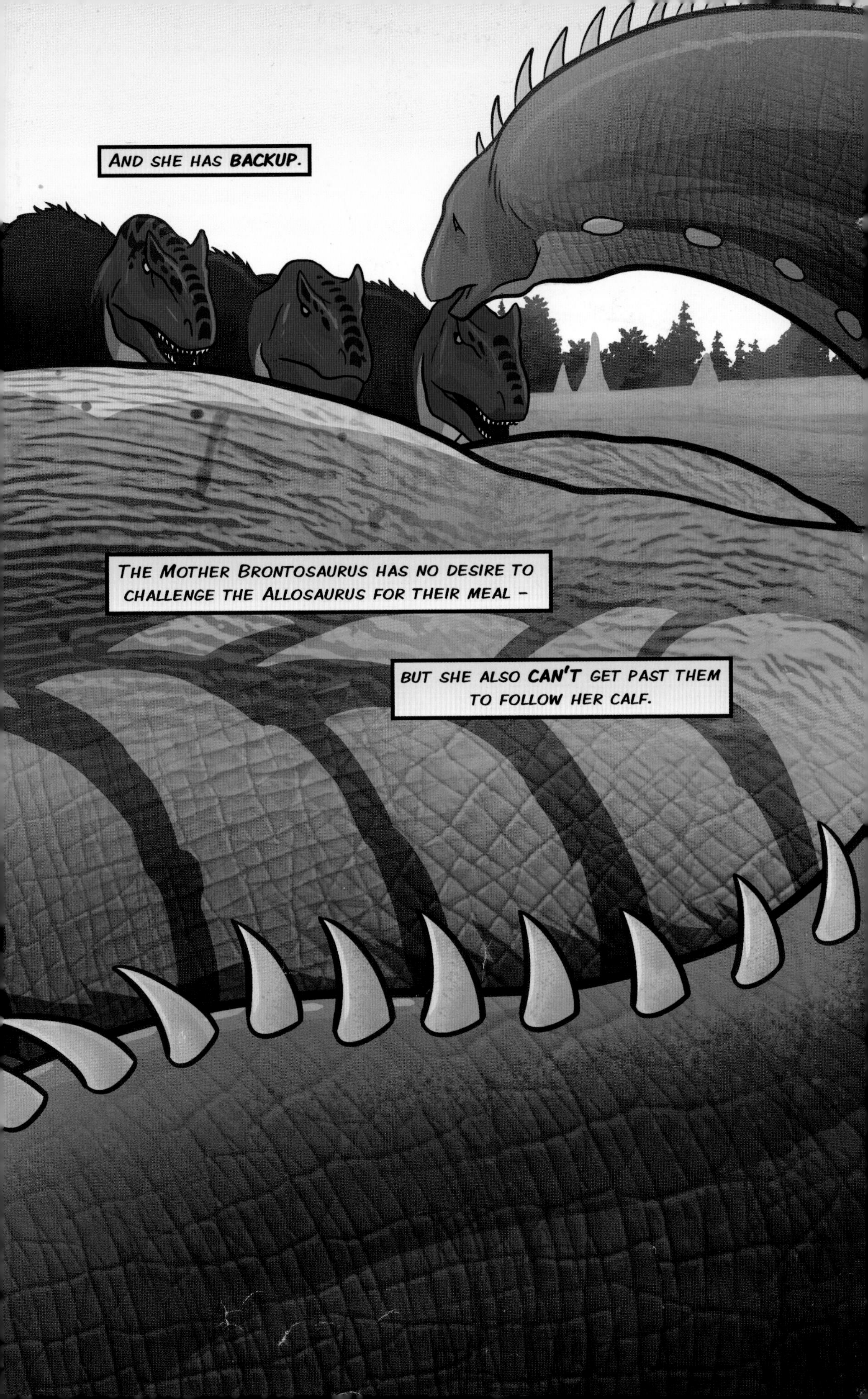
AND SHE HAS BACKUP.
THE MOTHER BRONTOSAURUS HAS NO DESIRE TO CHALLENGE THE ALLOSAURUS FOR THEIR MEAL –
BUT SHE ALSO CAN'T GET PAST THEM TO FOLLOW HER CALF.

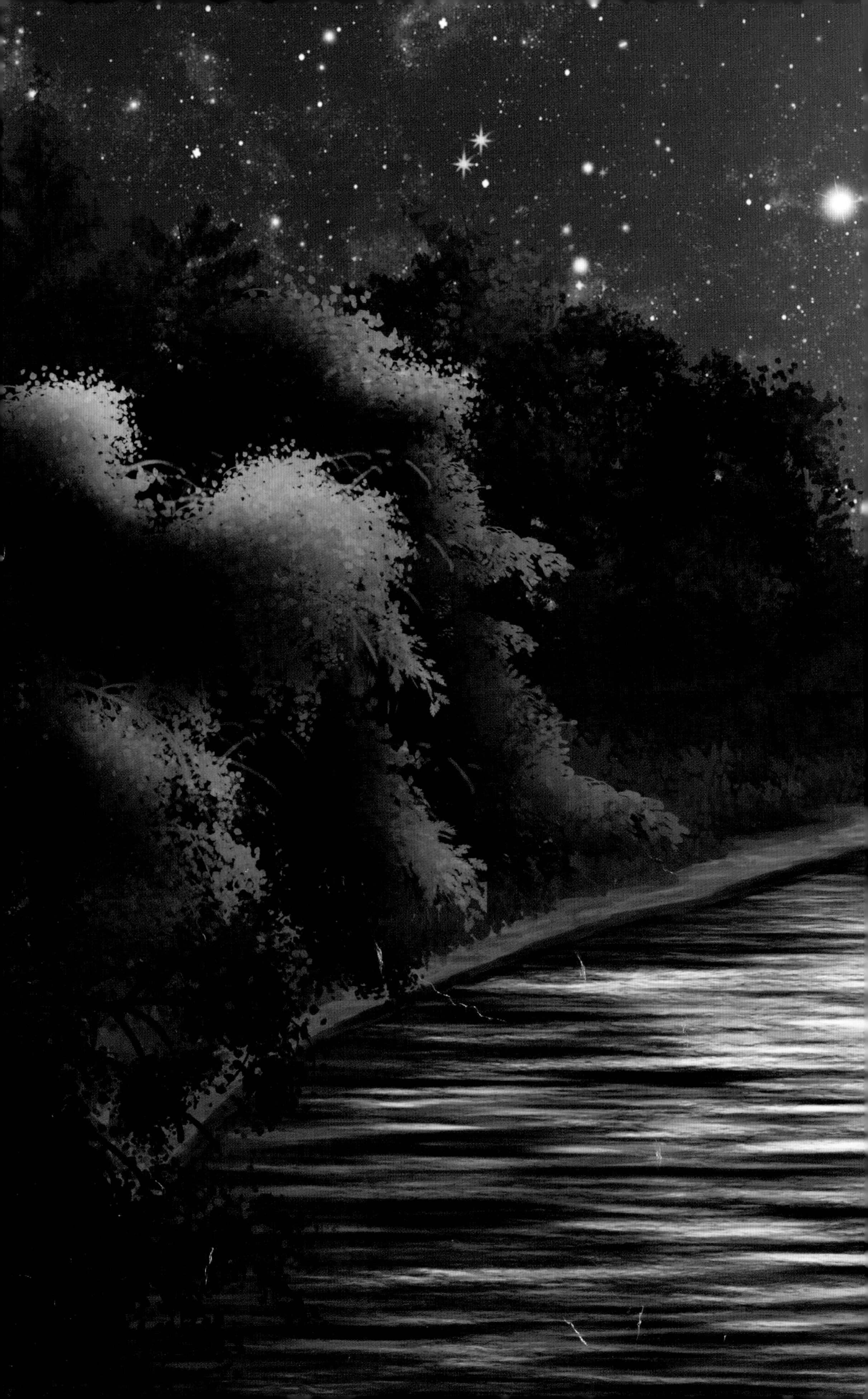

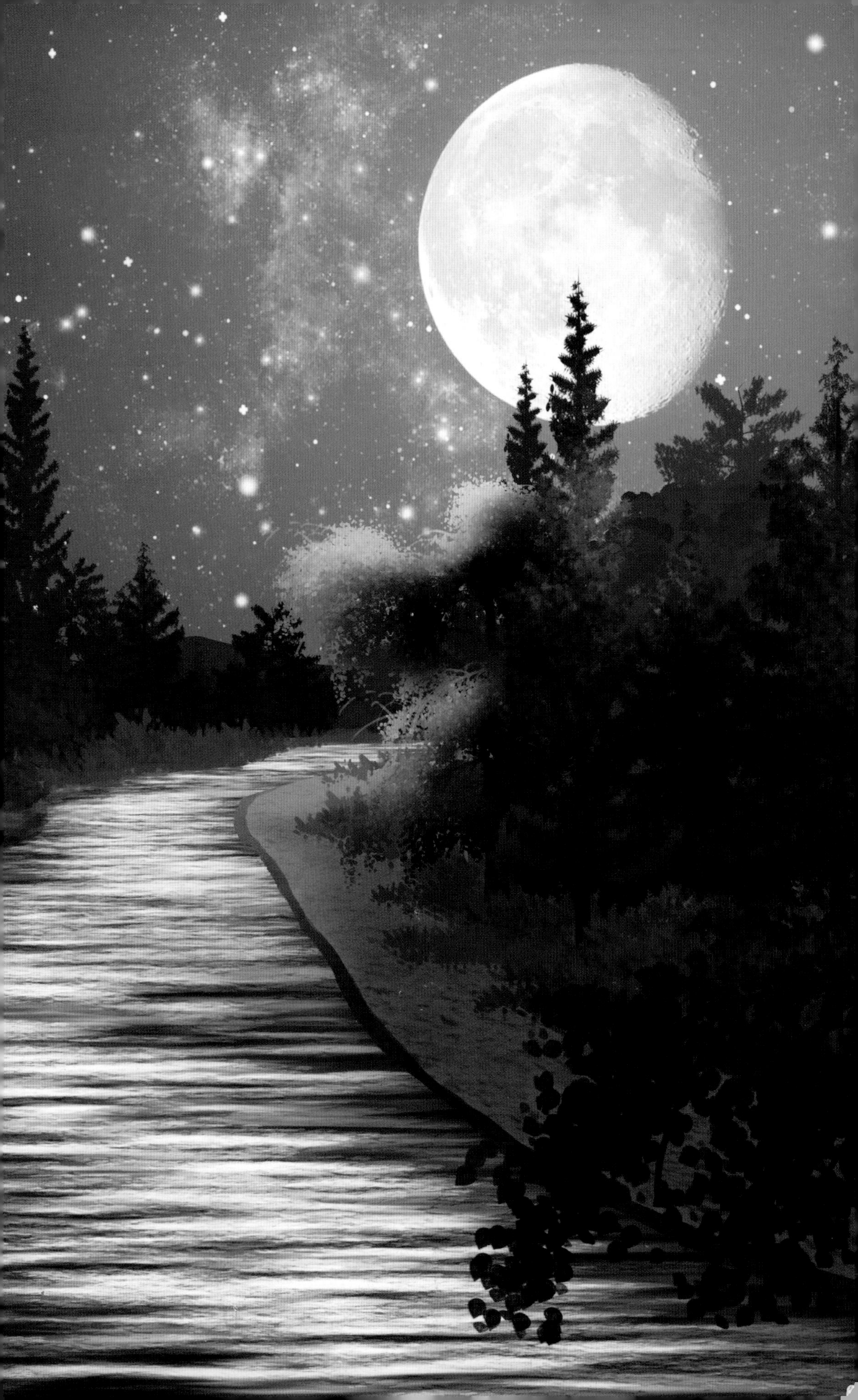

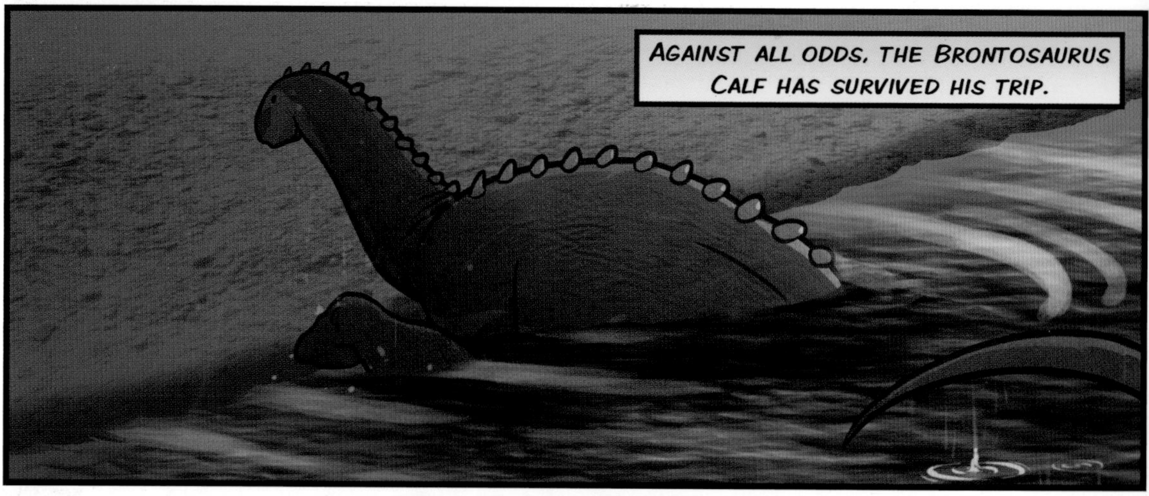
AGAINST ALL ODDS, THE BRONTOSAURUS CALF HAS SURVIVED HIS TRIP.

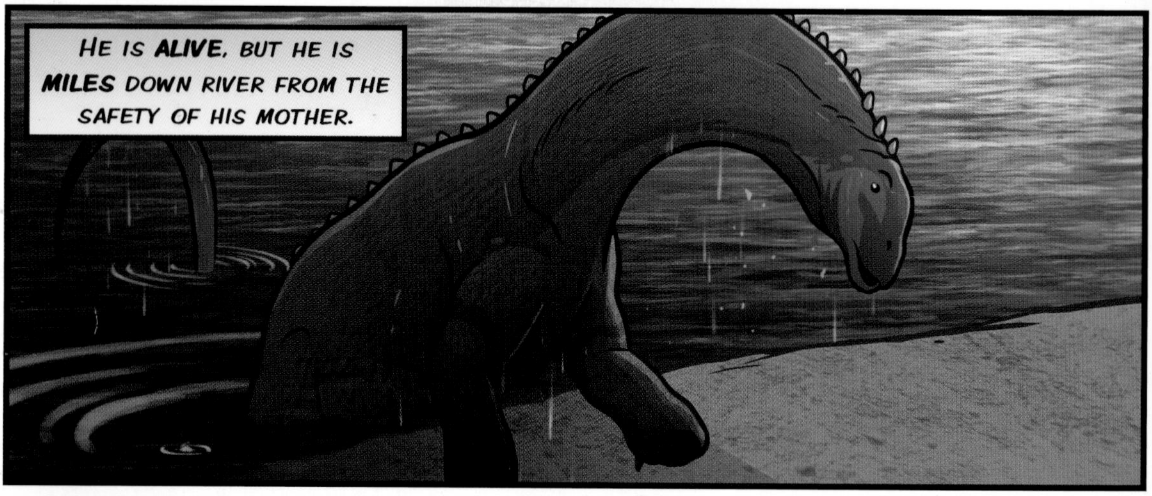
HE IS ALIVE, BUT HE IS MILES DOWN RIVER FROM THE SAFETY OF HIS MOTHER.

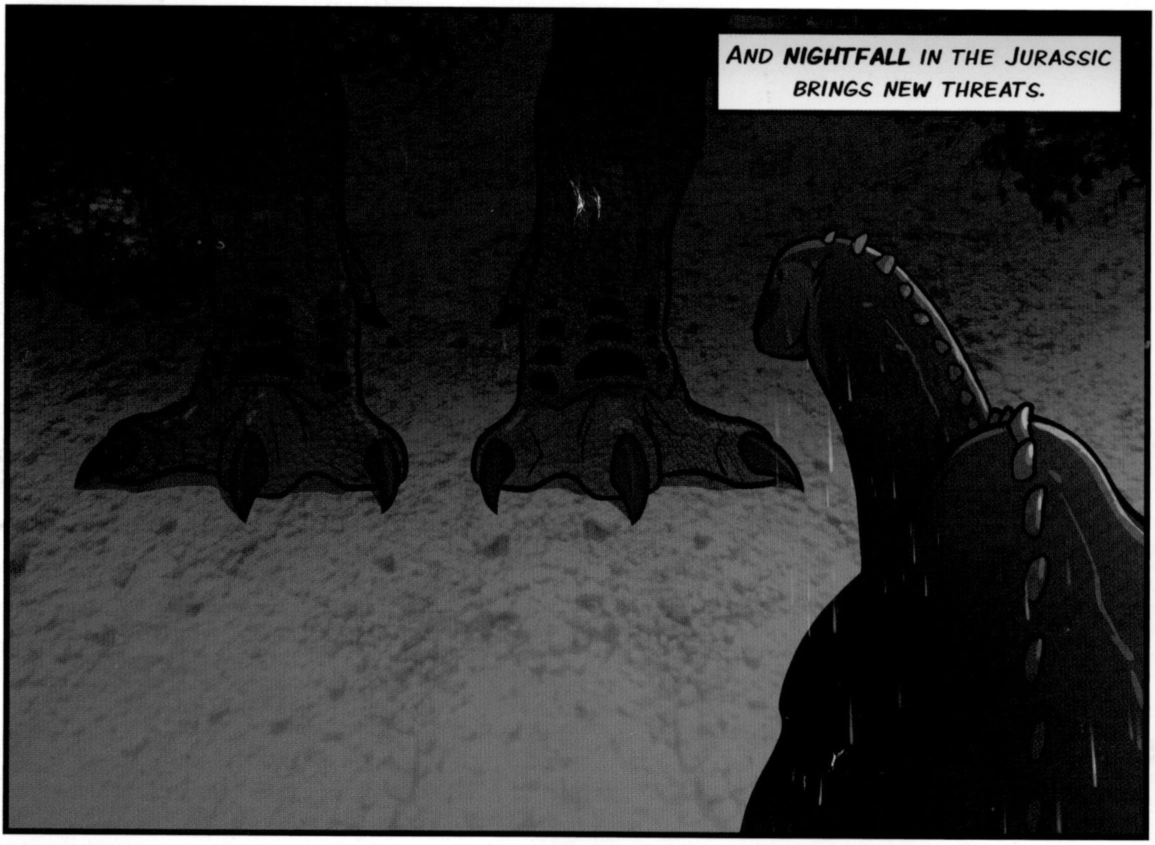
AND NIGHTFALL IN THE JURASSIC BRINGS NEW THREATS.

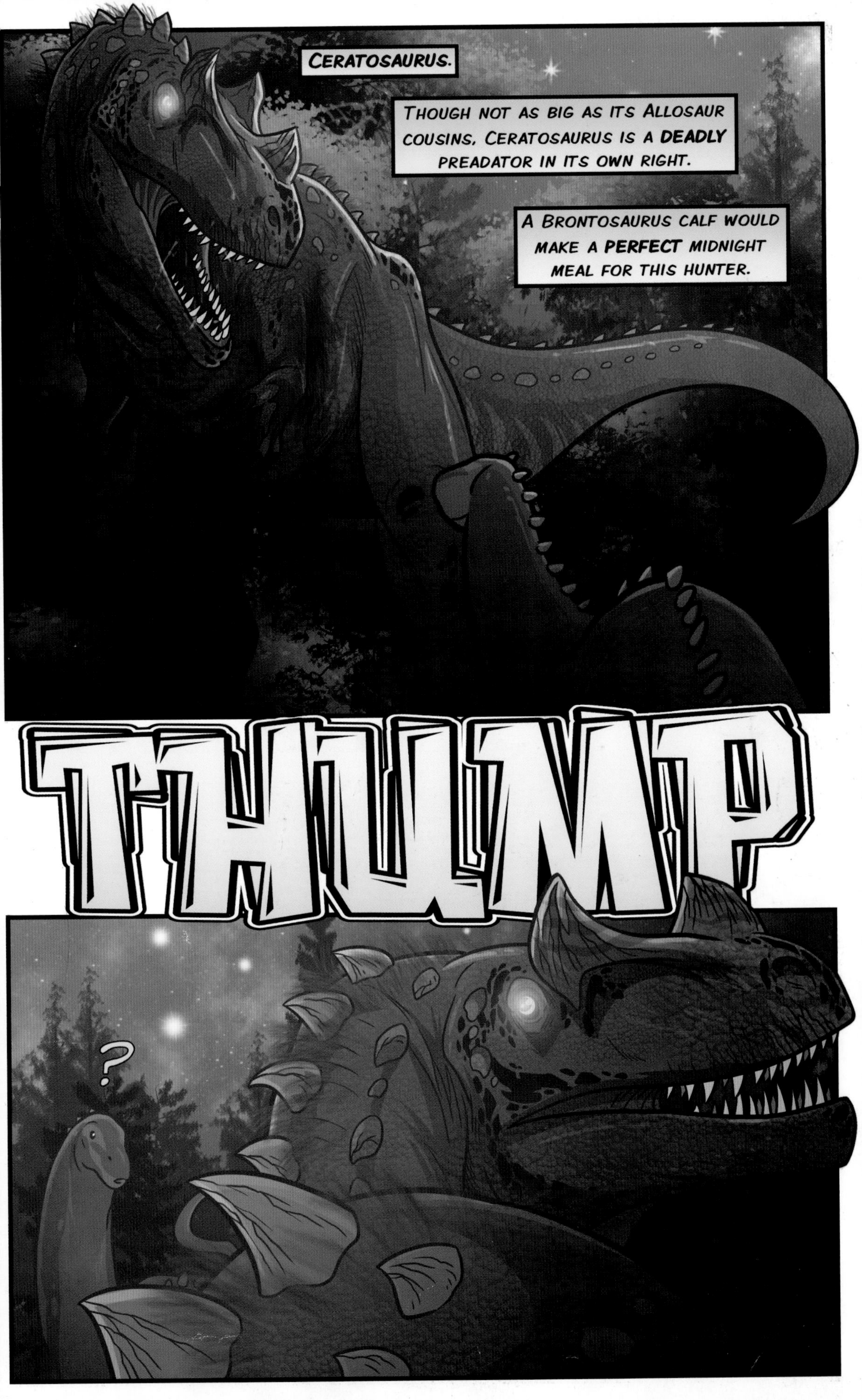
CERATOSAURUS.
THOUGH NOT AS BIG AS ITS ALLOSAUR COUSINS, CERATOSAURUS IS A DEADLY PREADATOR IN ITS OWN RIGHT.
A BRONTOSAURUS CALF WOULD MAKE A PERFECT MIDNIGHT MEAL FOR THIS HUNTER.
THUMP
?

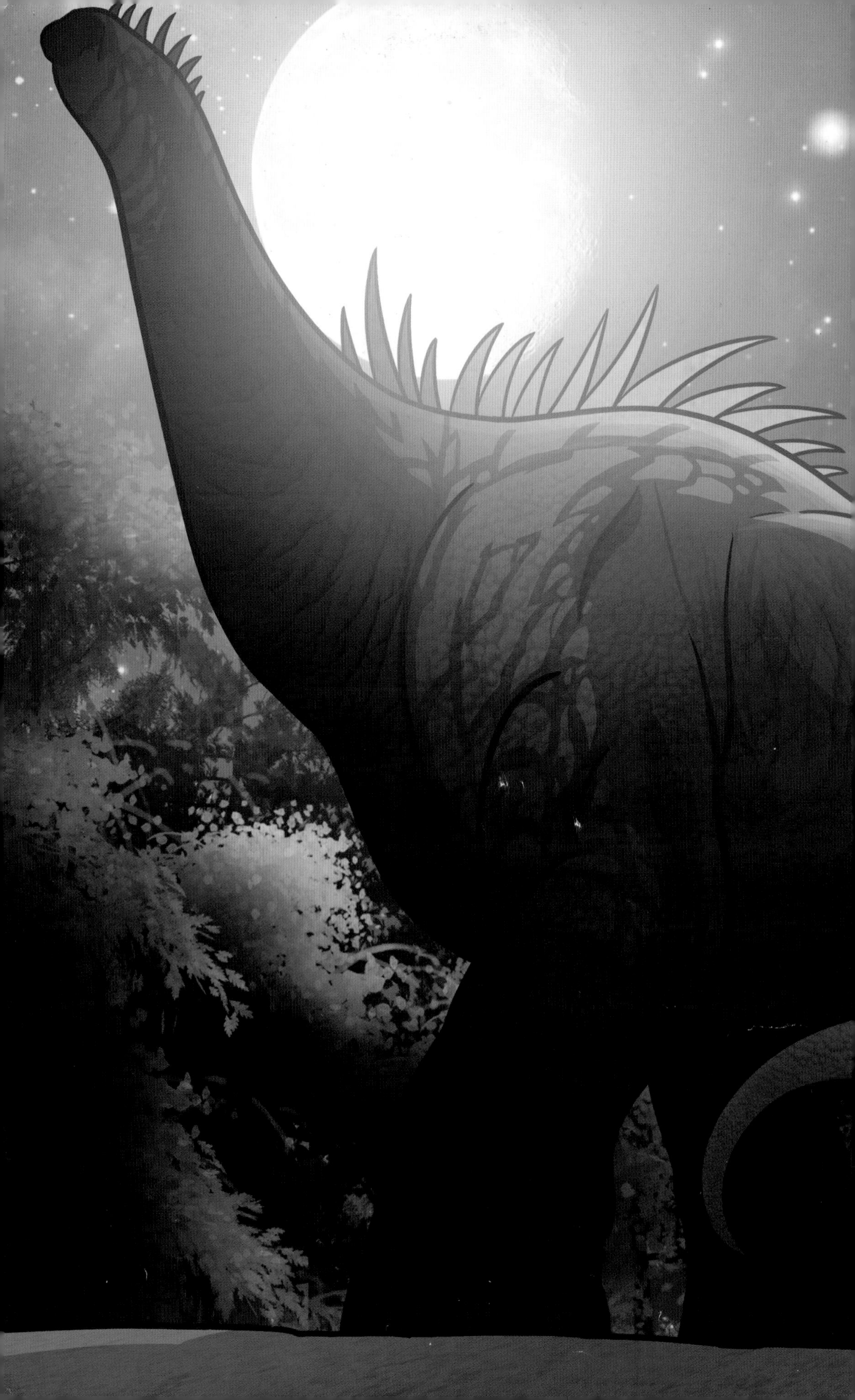

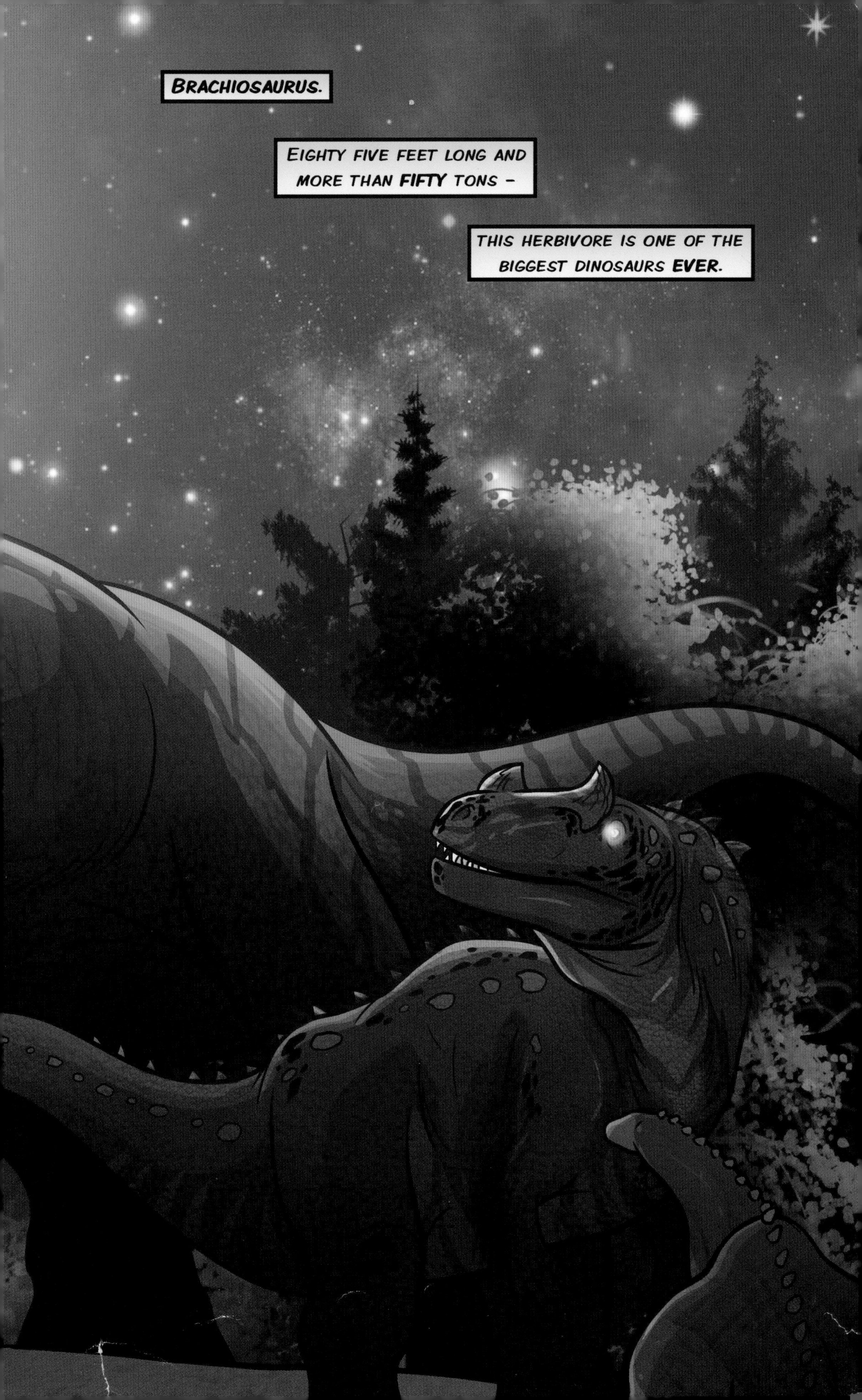
BRACHIOSAURUS.
EIGHTY FIVE FEET LONG AND MORE THAN FIFTY TONS –
THIS HERBIVORE IS ONE OF THE BIGGEST DINOSAURS EVER.

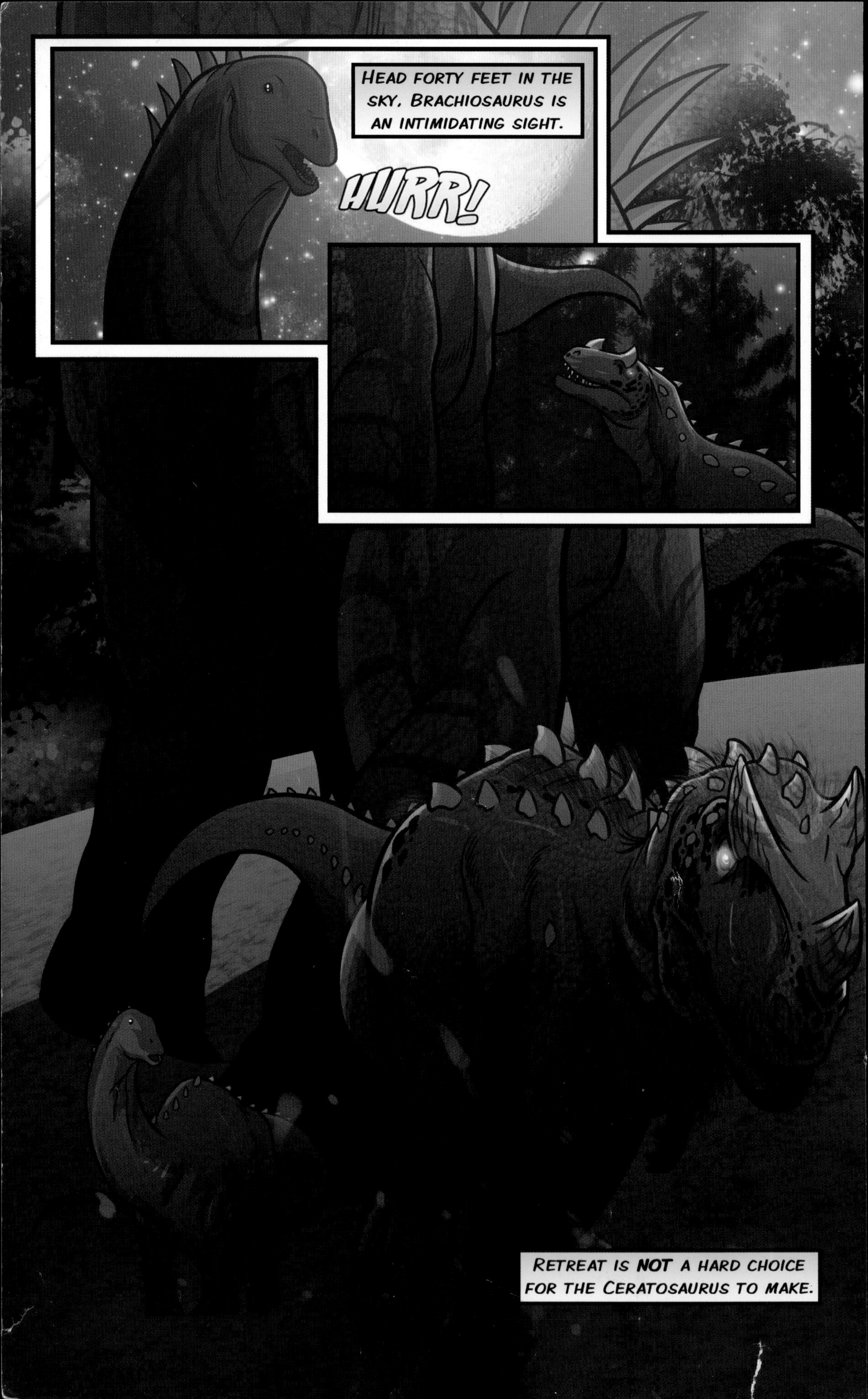
HEAD FORTY FEET IN THE SKY, BRACHIOSAURUS IS AN INTIMIDATING SIGHT.
HURR!
RETREAT IS NOT A HARD CHOICE FOR THE CERATOSAURUS TO MAKE.

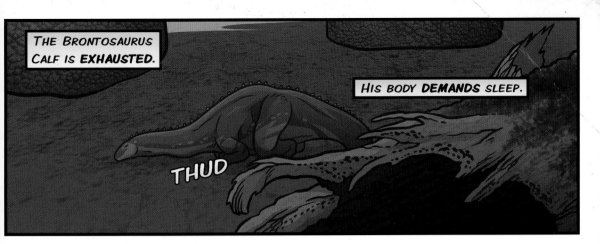

THE BRONTOSAURUS CALF IS **EXHAUSTED**.

HIS BODY **DEMANDS** SLEEP.

THUD

THOOM

GAH!

BUT MAYBE IN A SAFER SPOT.

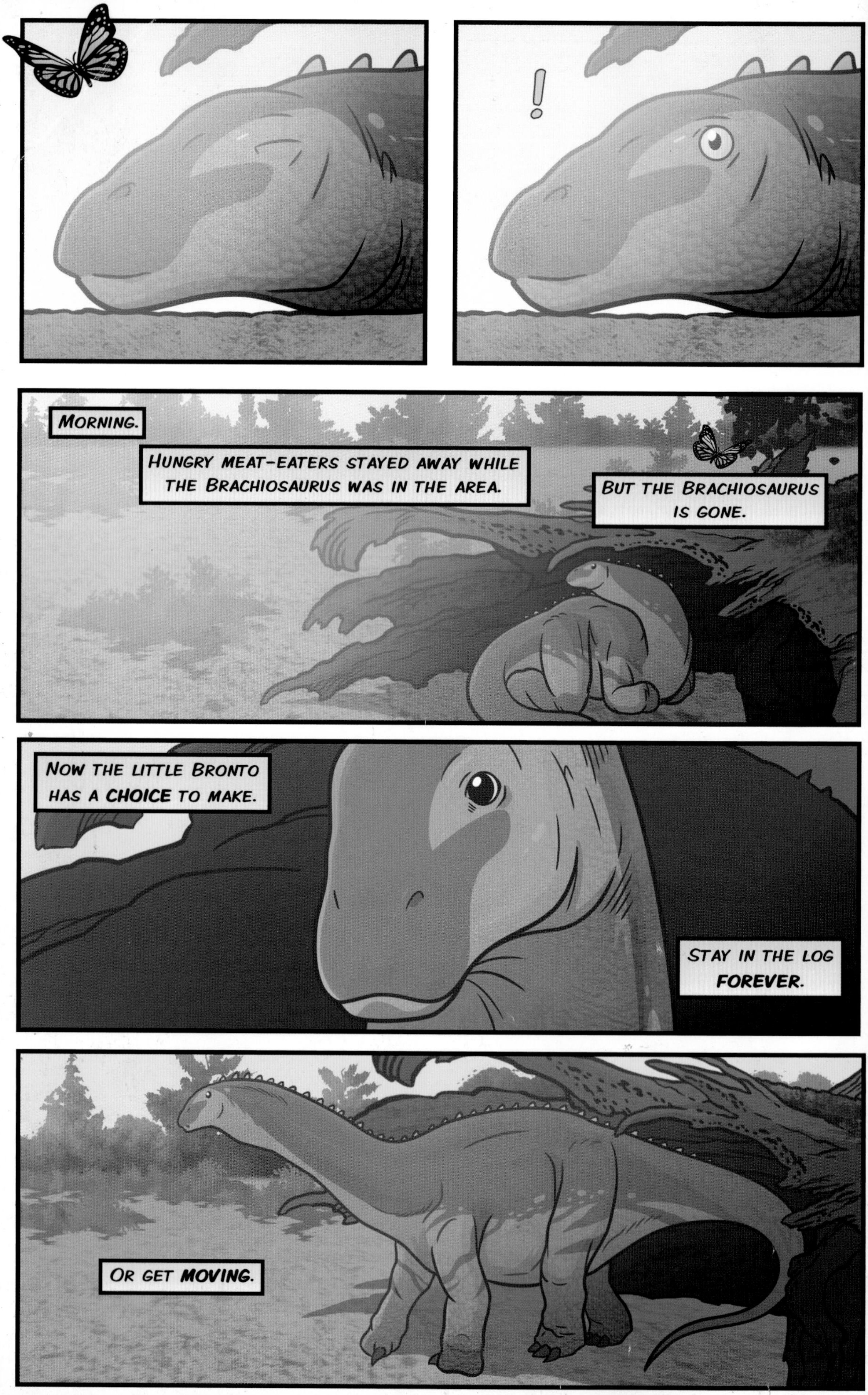
!
MORNING.
HUNGRY MEAT-EATERS STAYED AWAY WHILE THE BRACHIOSAURUS WAS IN THE AREA.
BUT THE BRACHIOSAURUS IS GONE.
NOW THE LITTLE BRONTO HAS A CHOICE TO MAKE.
STAY IN THE LOG FOREVER.
OR GET MOVING.

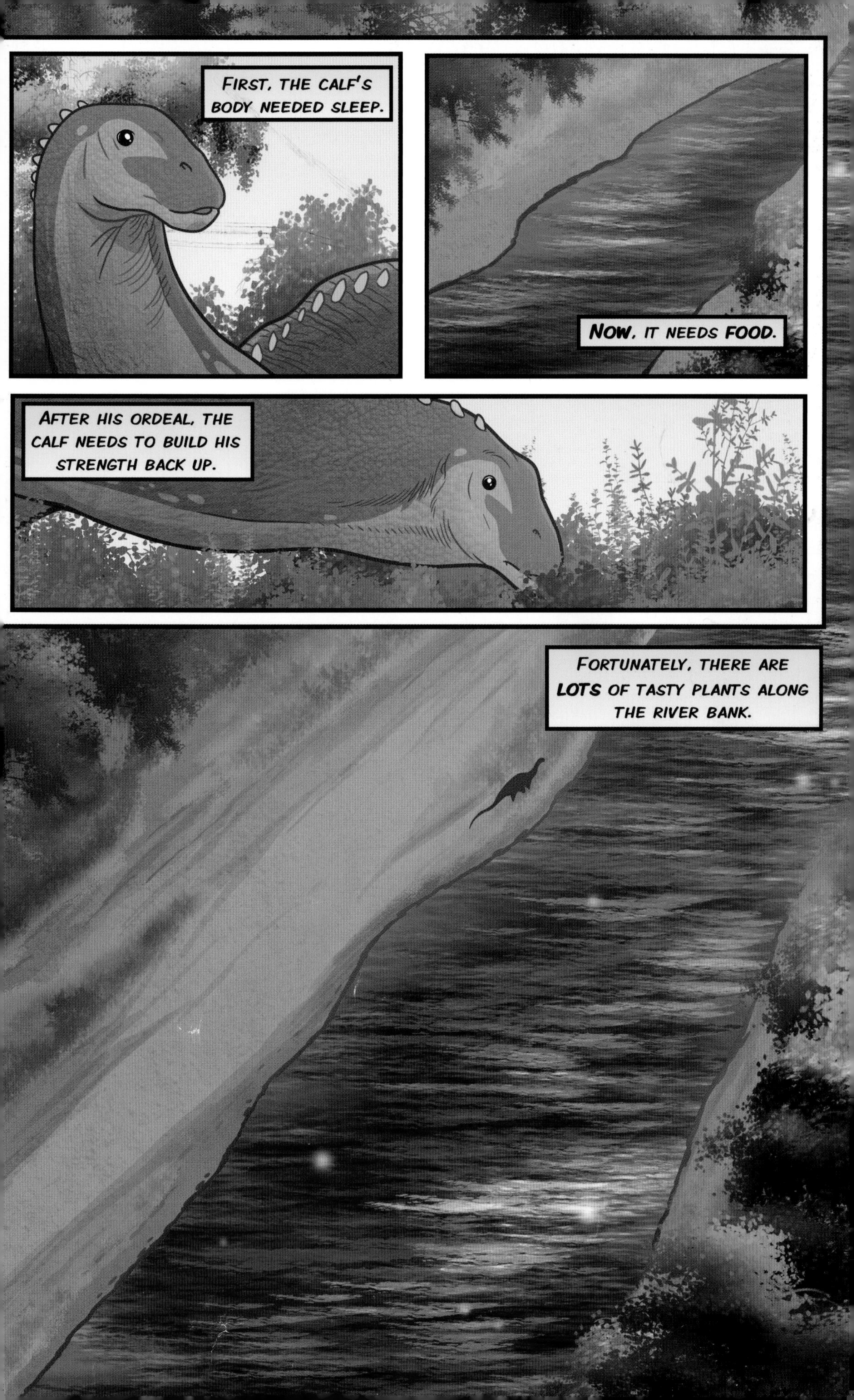
FIRST, THE CALF'S BODY NEEDED SLEEP.
NOW, IT NEEDS FOOD.
AFTER HIS ORDEAL, THE CALF NEEDS TO BUILD HIS STRENGTH BACK UP.
FORTUNATELY, THERE ARE LOTS OF TASTY PLANTS ALONG THE RIVER BANK.

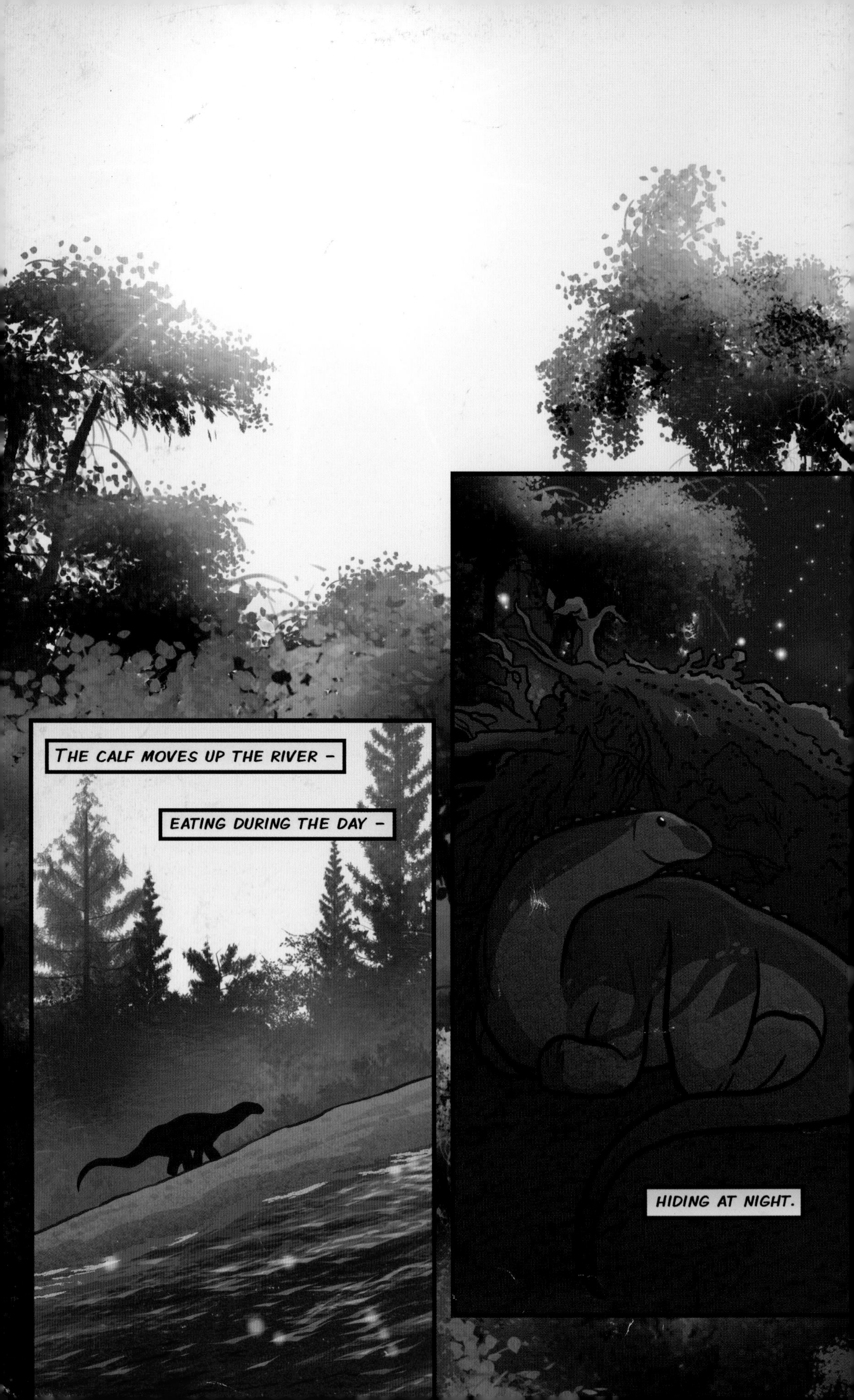
THE CALF MOVES UP THE RIVER –
EATING DURING THE DAY –
HIDING AT NIGHT.

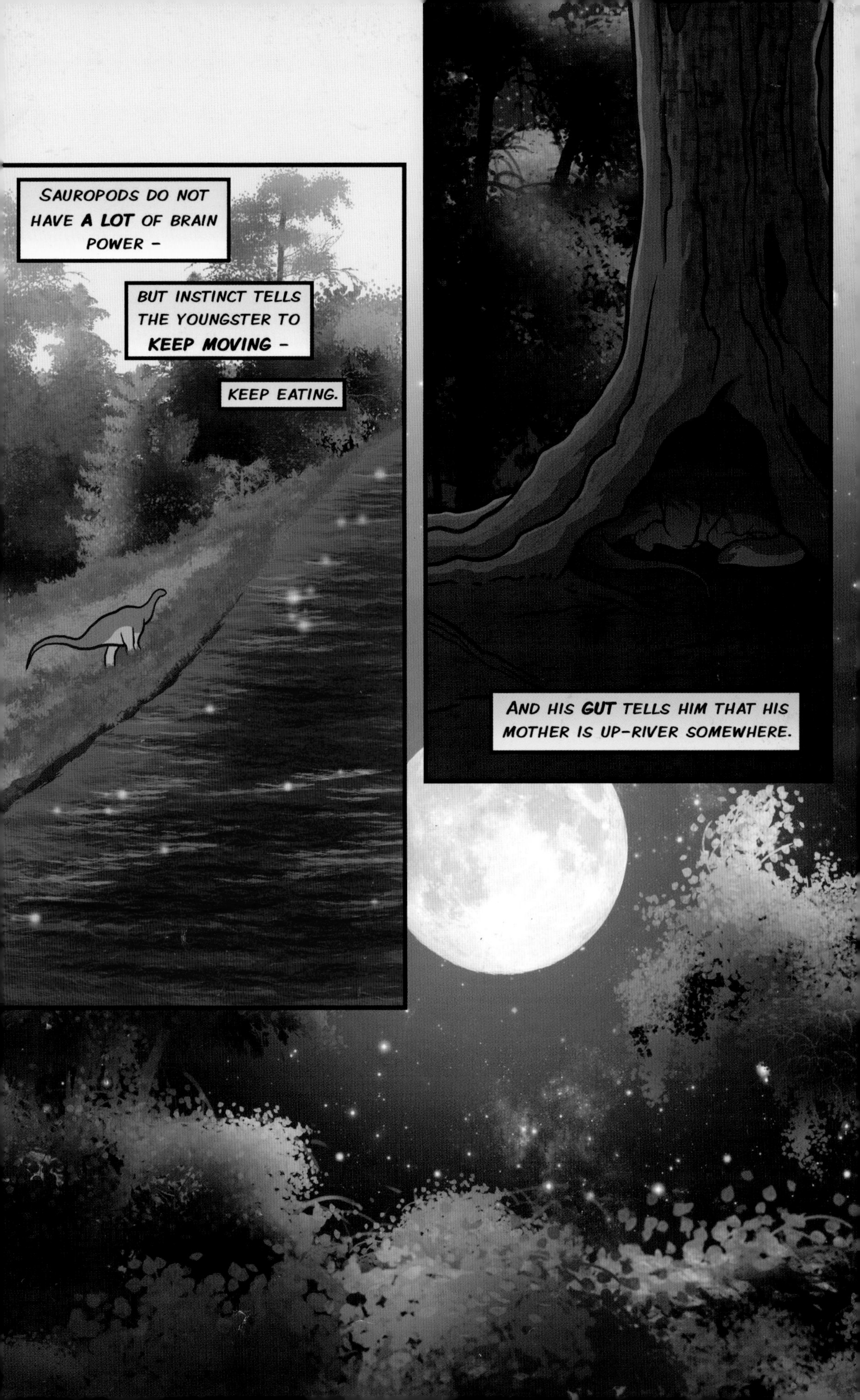
SAUROPODS DO NOT HAVE A LOT OF BRAIN POWER -
BUT INSTINCT TELLS THE YOUNGSTER TO KEEP MOVING -
KEEP EATING.
AND HIS GUT TELLS HIM THAT HIS MOTHER IS UP-RIVER SOMEWHERE.

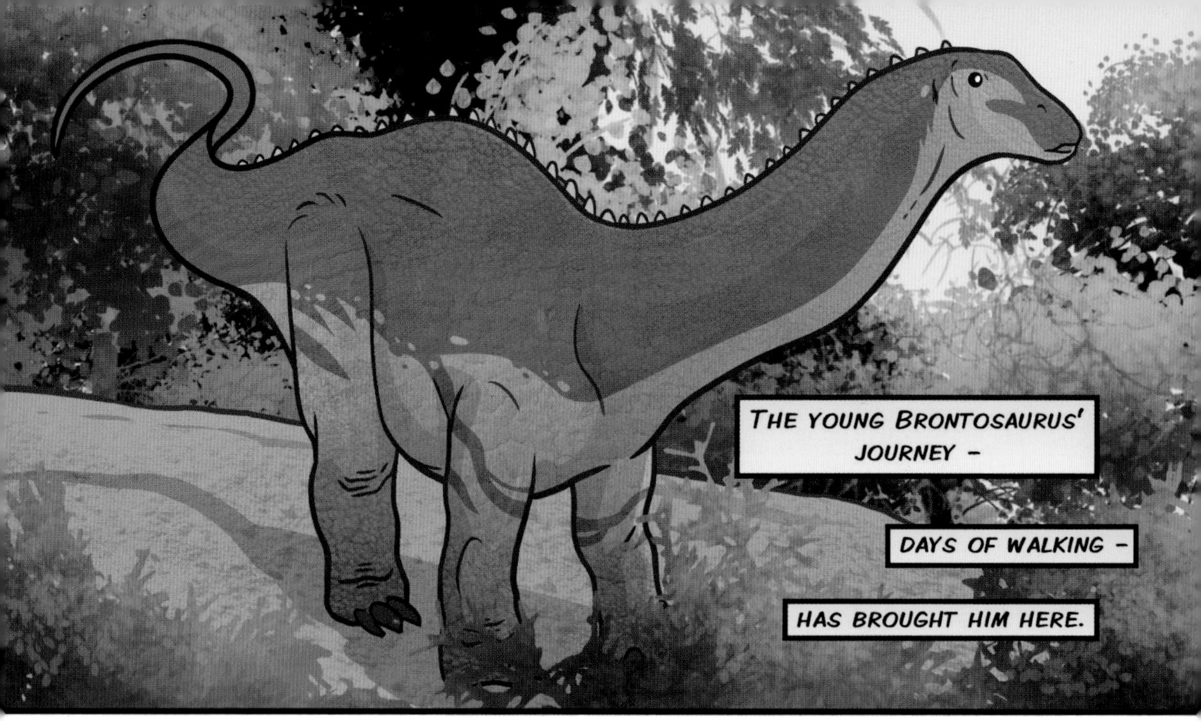
THE YOUNG BRONTOSAURUS' JOURNEY –
DAYS OF WALKING –
HAS BROUGHT HIM HERE.

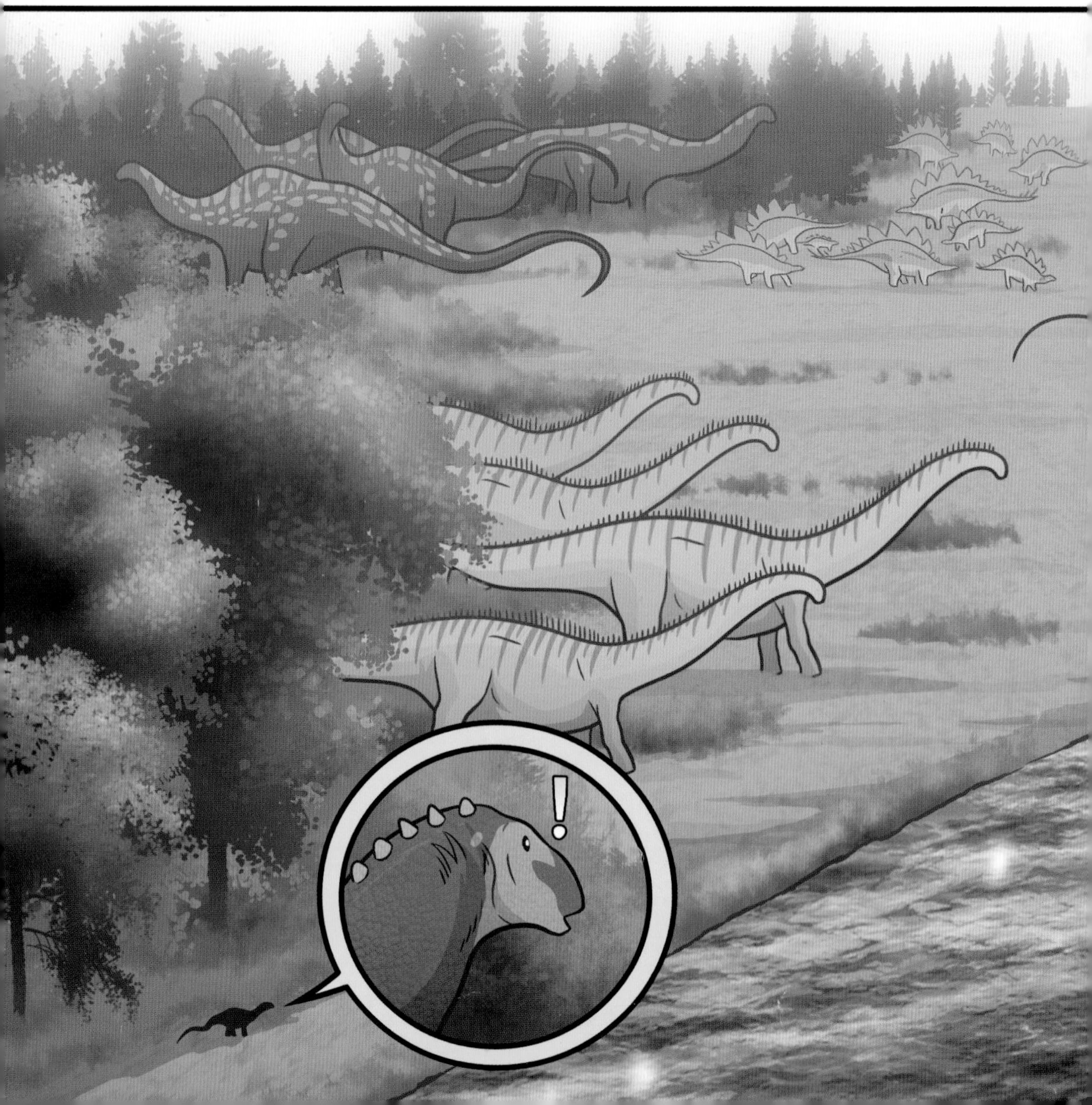
!

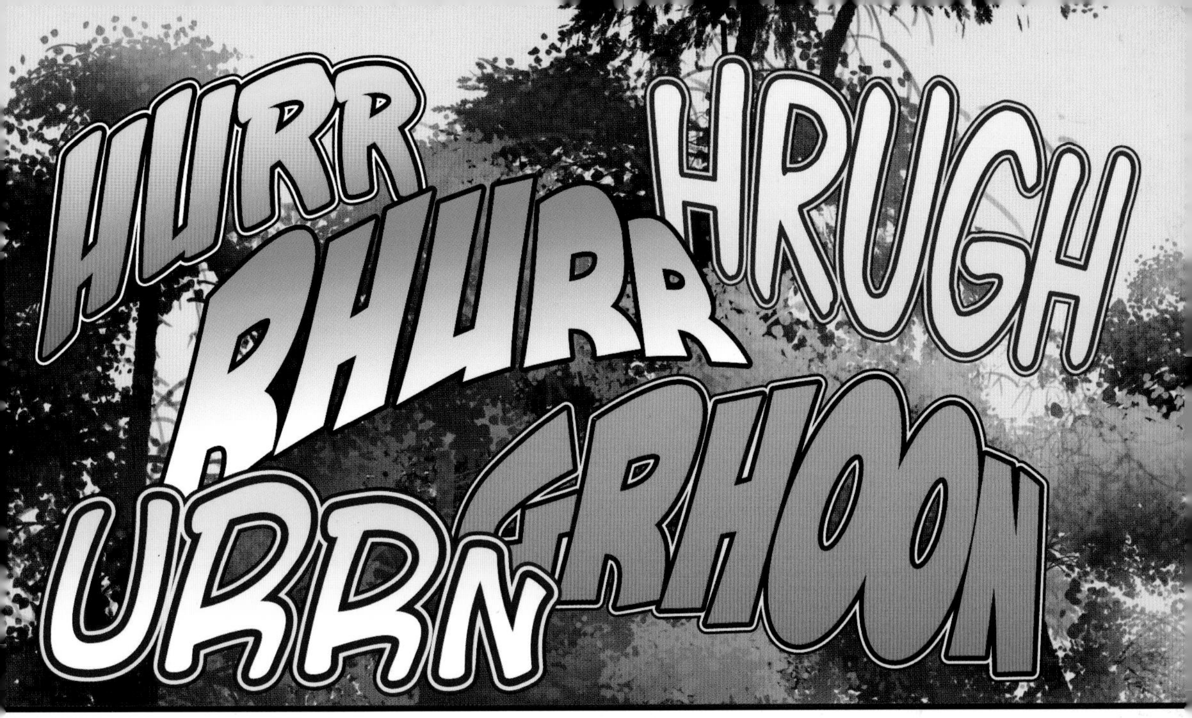
HURR
RHURR
HRUGH
URRN
GRHOON

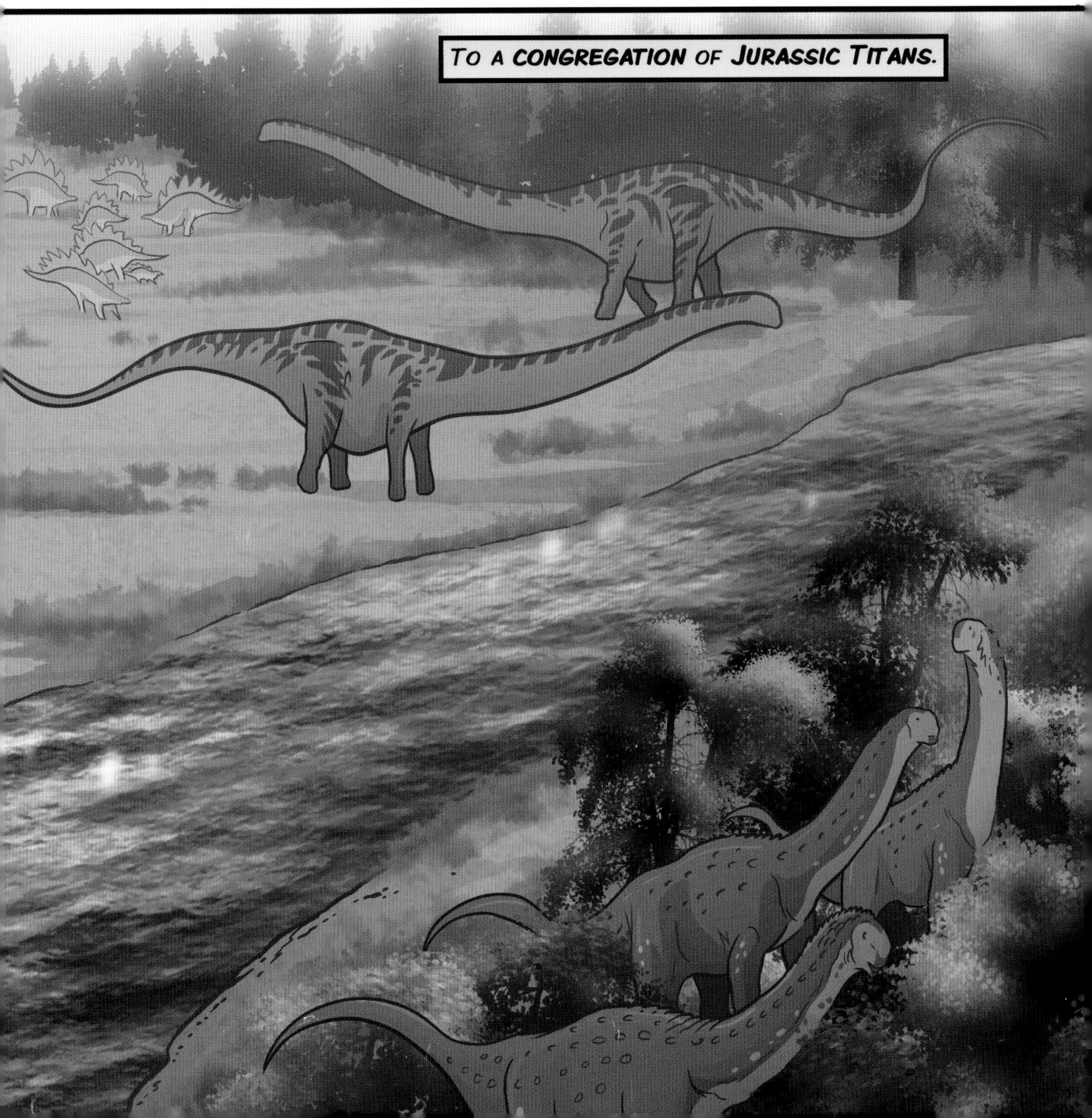
TO A CONGREGATION OF JURASSIC TITANS.

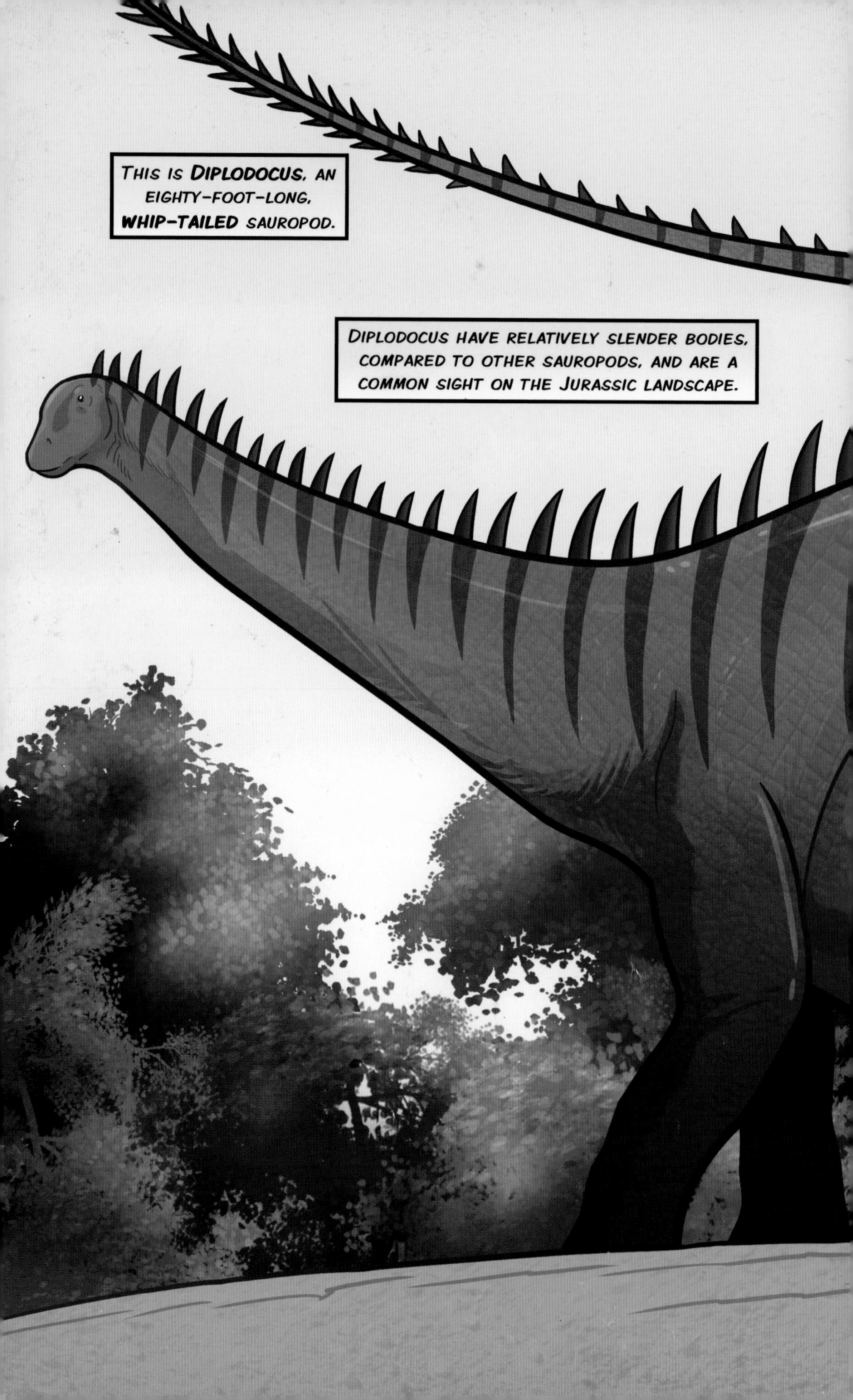
THIS IS DIPLODOCUS, AN EIGHTY-FOOT-LONG, WHIP-TAILED SAUROPOD.
DIPLODOCUS HAVE RELATIVELY SLENDER BODIES, COMPARED TO OTHER SAUROPODS, AND ARE A COMMON SIGHT ON THE JURASSIC LANDSCAPE.

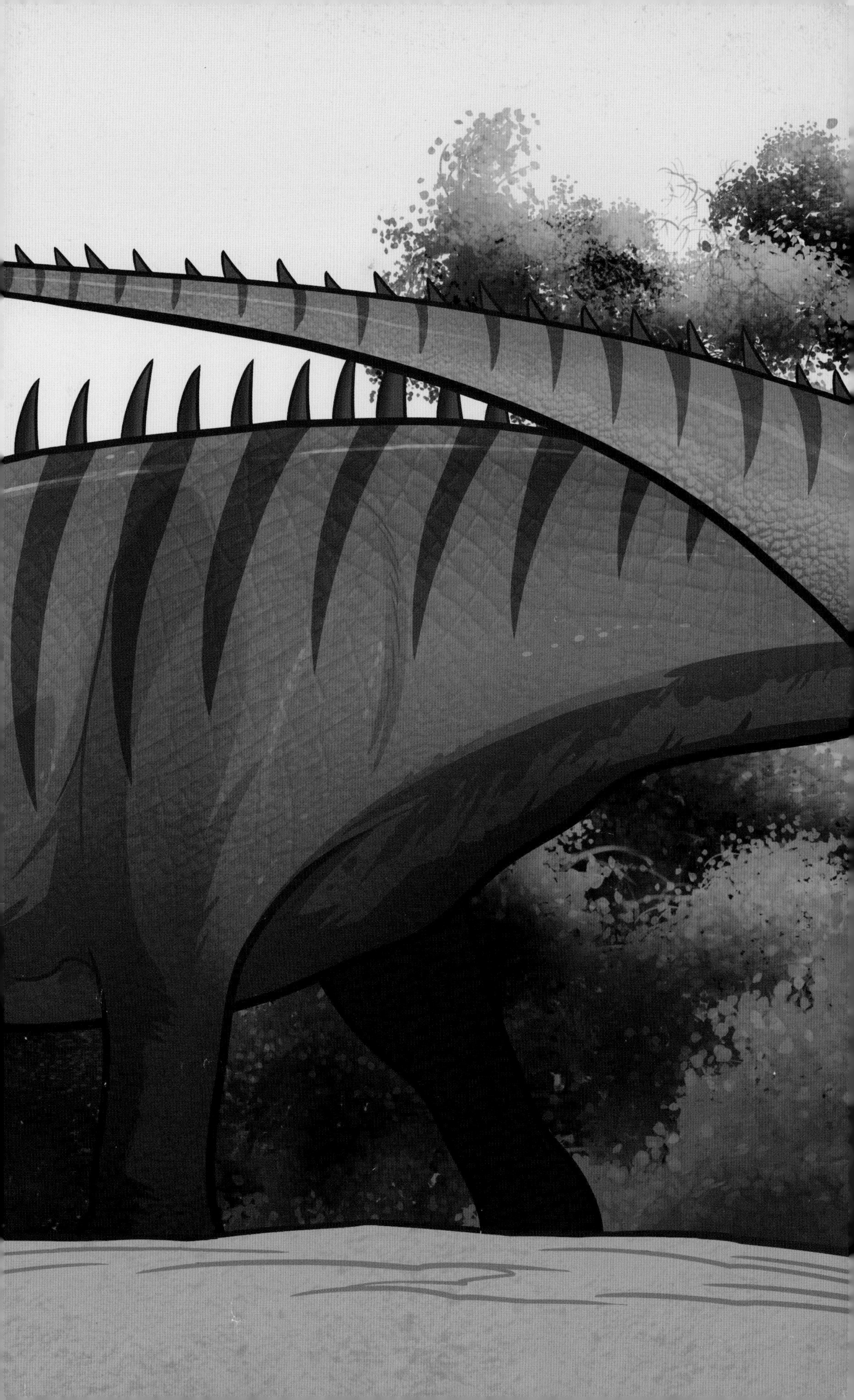

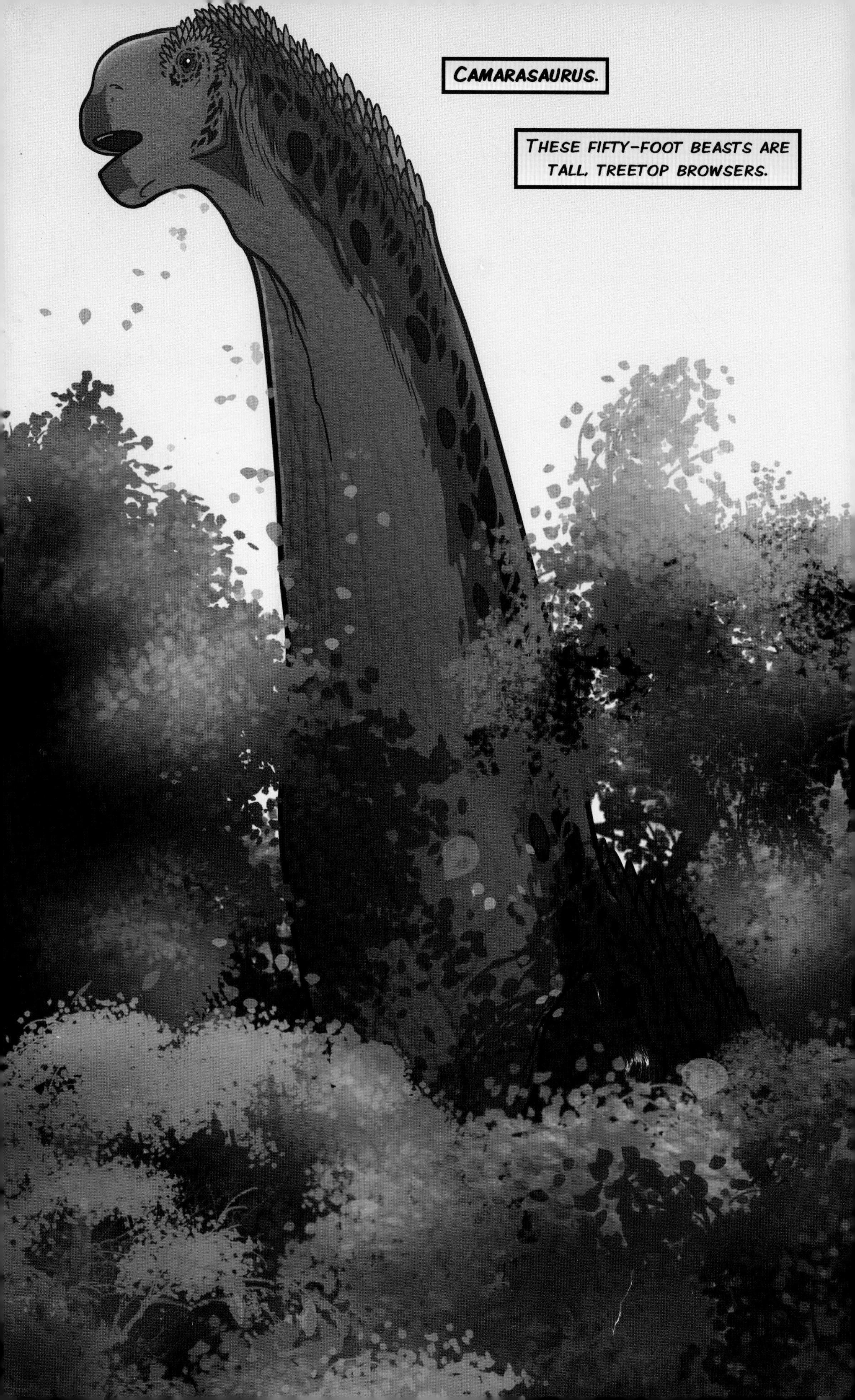
CAMARASAURUS.
THESE FIFTY-FOOT BEASTS ARE TALL, TREETOP BROWSERS.

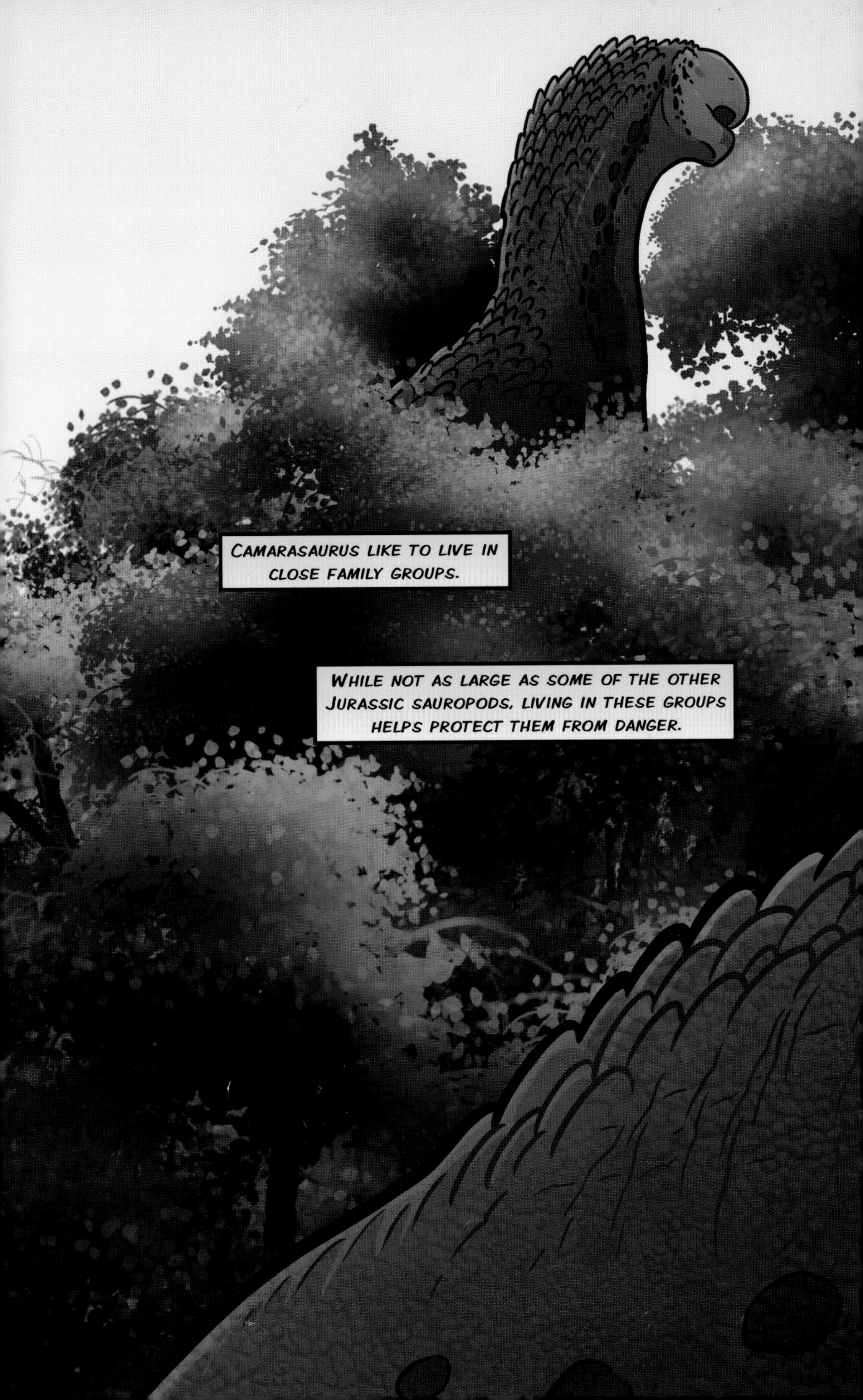
Camarasaurus like to live in close family groups.
While not as large as some of the other Jurassic sauropods, living in these groups helps protect them from danger.

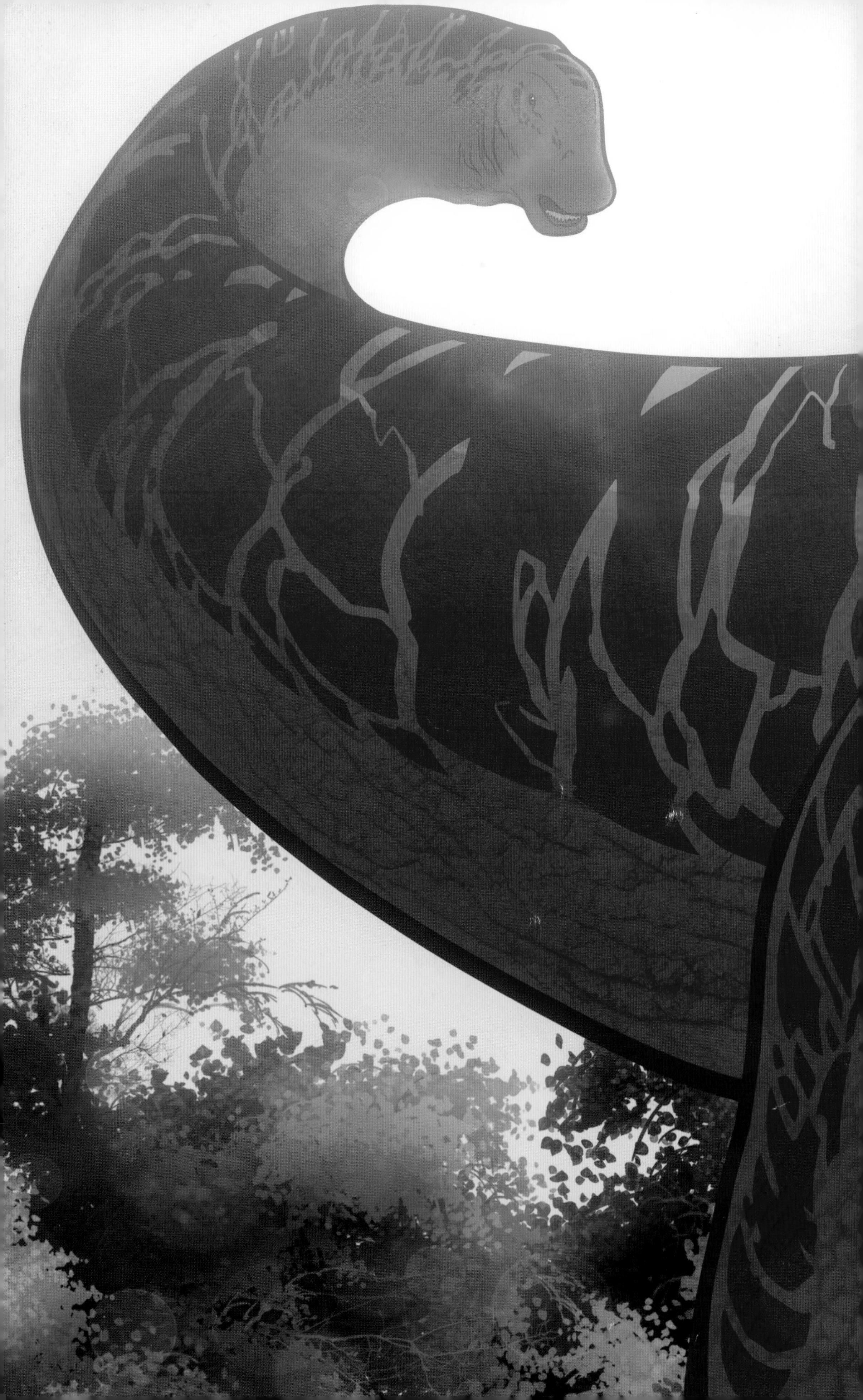

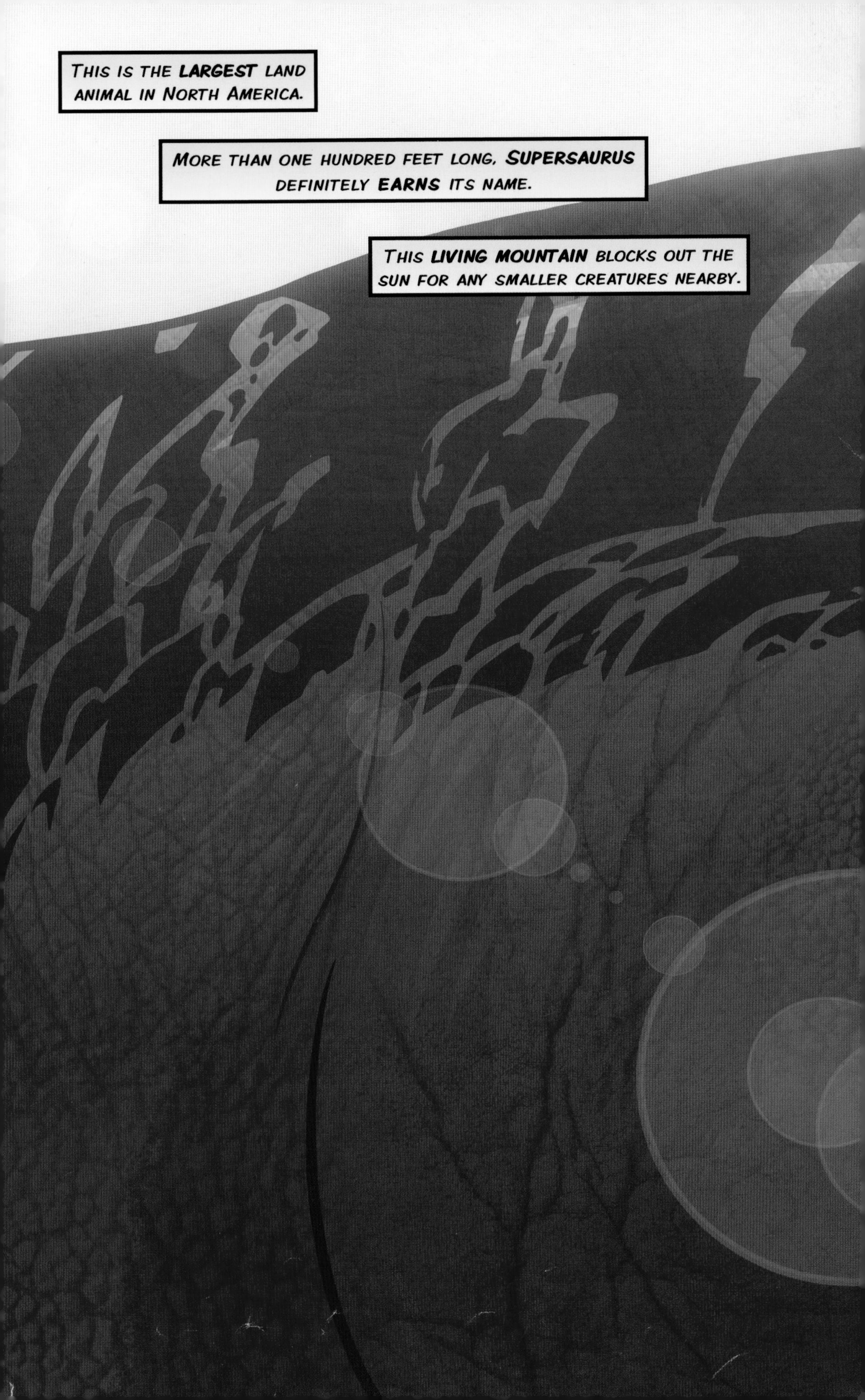
THIS IS THE LARGEST LAND ANIMAL IN NORTH AMERICA.
MORE THAN ONE HUNDRED FEET LONG, SUPERSAURUS DEFINITELY EARNS ITS NAME.
THIS LIVING MOUNTAIN BLOCKS OUT THE SUN FOR ANY SMALLER CREATURES NEARBY.

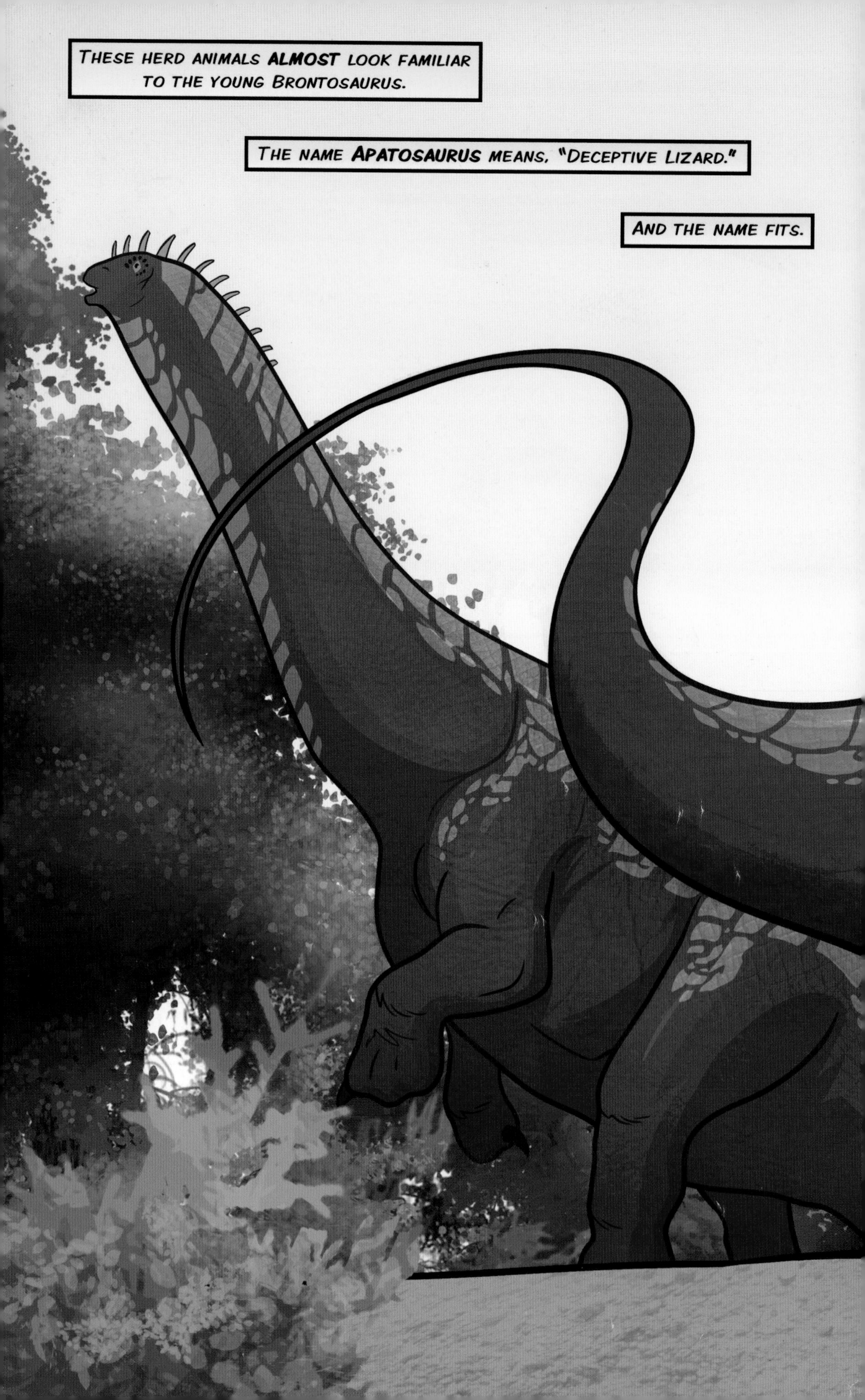
These herd animals ALMOST look familiar to the young Brontosaurus.
The name APATOSAURUS means, "Deceptive Lizard."
And the name fits.

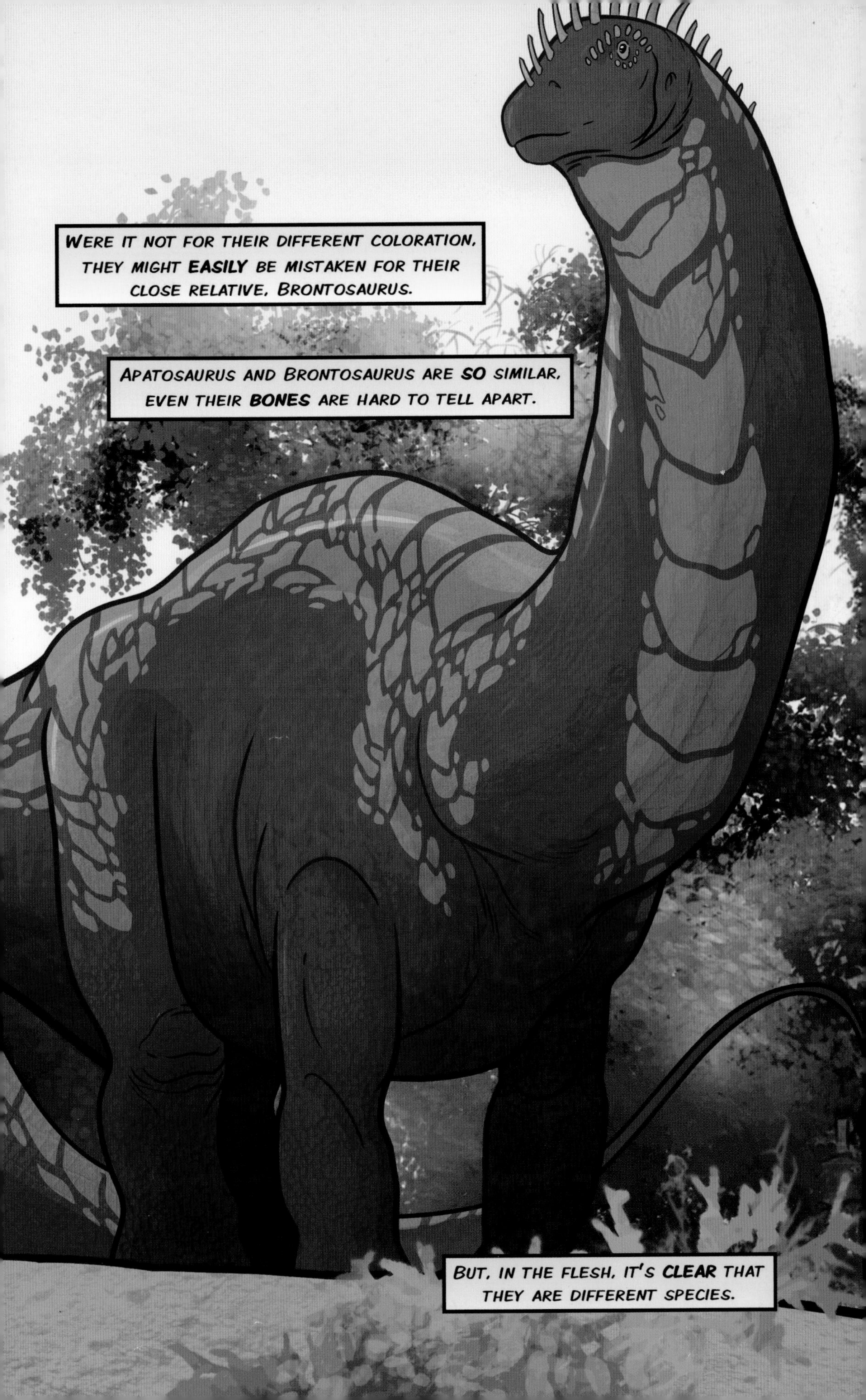
WERE IT NOT FOR THEIR DIFFERENT COLORATION, THEY MIGHT EASILY BE MISTAKEN FOR THEIR CLOSE RELATIVE, BRONTOSAURUS.
APATOSAURUS AND BRONTOSAURUS ARE SO SIMILAR, EVEN THEIR BONES ARE HARD TO TELL APART.
BUT, IN THE FLESH, IT'S CLEAR THAT THEY ARE DIFFERENT SPECIES.

THE LITTLE BRONTOSAURUS' MOTHER IS NOWHERE IN SIGHT, SO HE KEEPS MOVING.

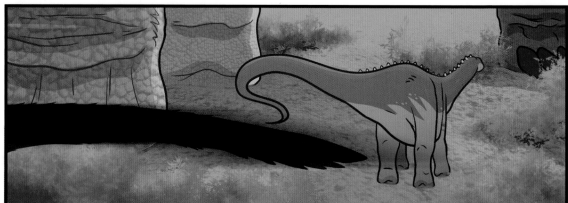

HE'S BEING **FOLLOWED.**

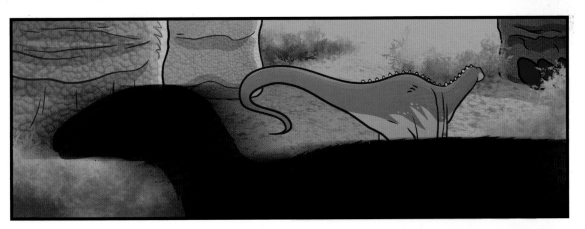

THE CALF IS **NOT ALONE** UNDER THE BELLIES OF THESE GIANTS.

ORNITHOLESTES.

TRANSLATION: TROUBLE.

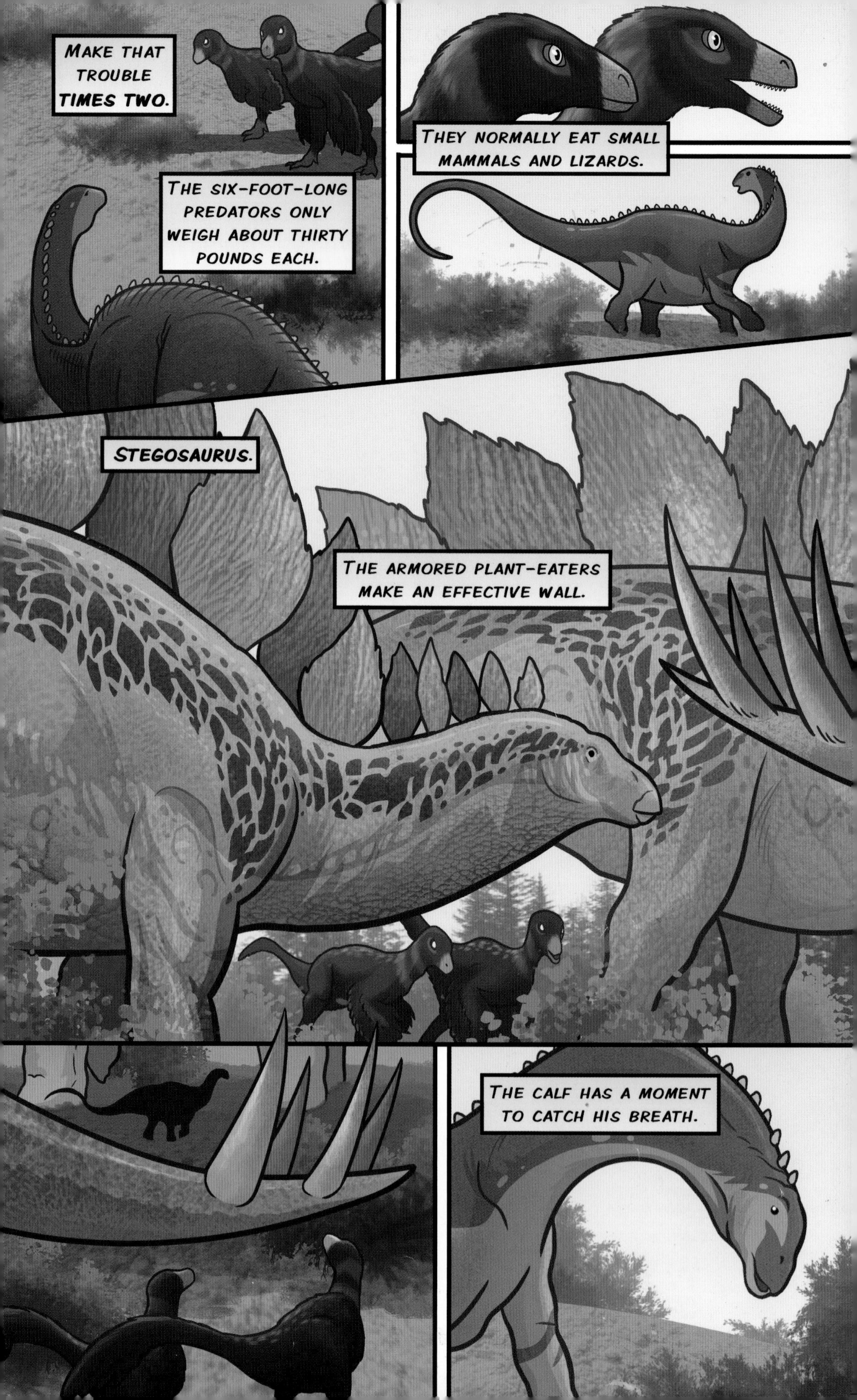
MAKE THAT TROUBLE TIMES TWO.
THEY NORMALLY EAT SMALL MAMMALS AND LIZARDS.
THE SIX-FOOT-LONG PREDATORS ONLY WEIGH ABOUT THIRTY POUNDS EACH.
STEGOSAURUS.
THE ARMORED PLANT-EATERS MAKE AN EFFECTIVE WALL.
THE CALF HAS A MOMENT TO CATCH HIS BREATH.

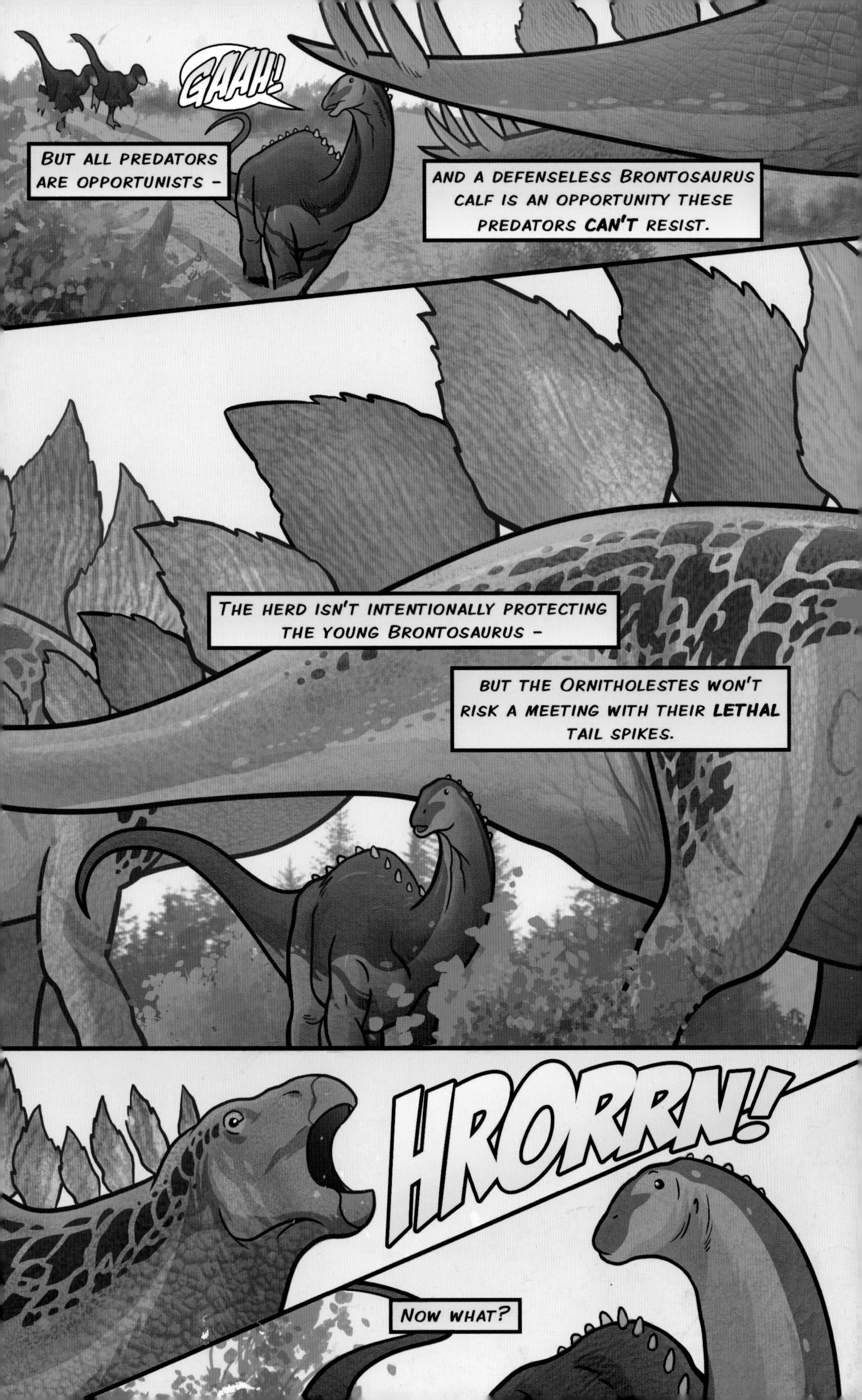
GAAAH!
BUT ALL PREDATORS ARE OPPORTUNISTS –
AND A DEFENSELESS BRONTOSAURUS CALF IS AN OPPORTUNITY THESE PREDATORS CAN'T RESIST.
THE HERD ISN'T INTENTIONALLY PROTECTING THE YOUNG BRONTOSAURUS –
BUT THE ORNITHOLESTES WON'T RISK A MEETING WITH THEIR LETHAL TAIL SPIKES.
HRORRRN!
NOW WHAT?

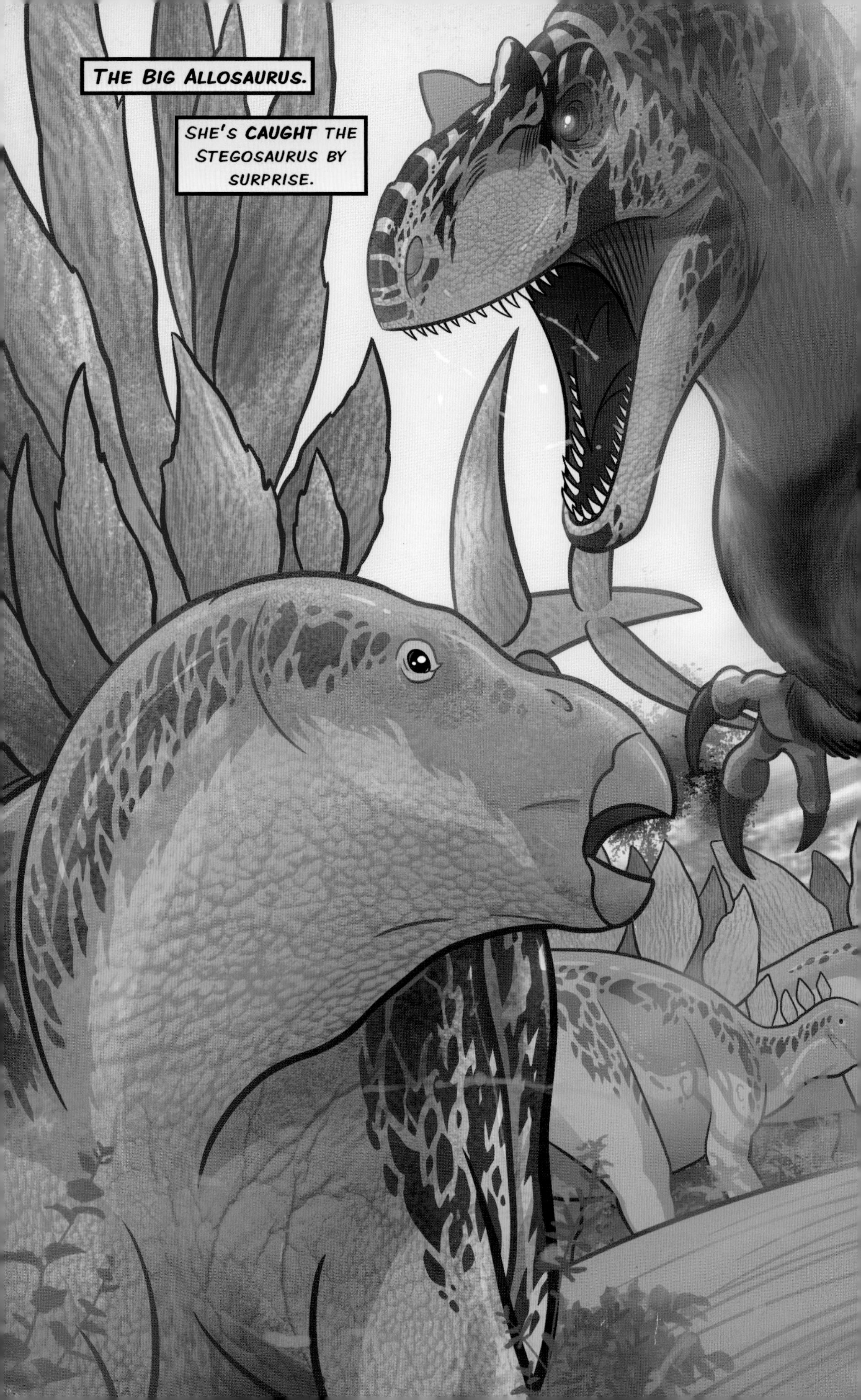
THE BIG ALLOSAURUS.
SHE'S CAUGHT THE STEGOSAURUS BY SURPRISE.

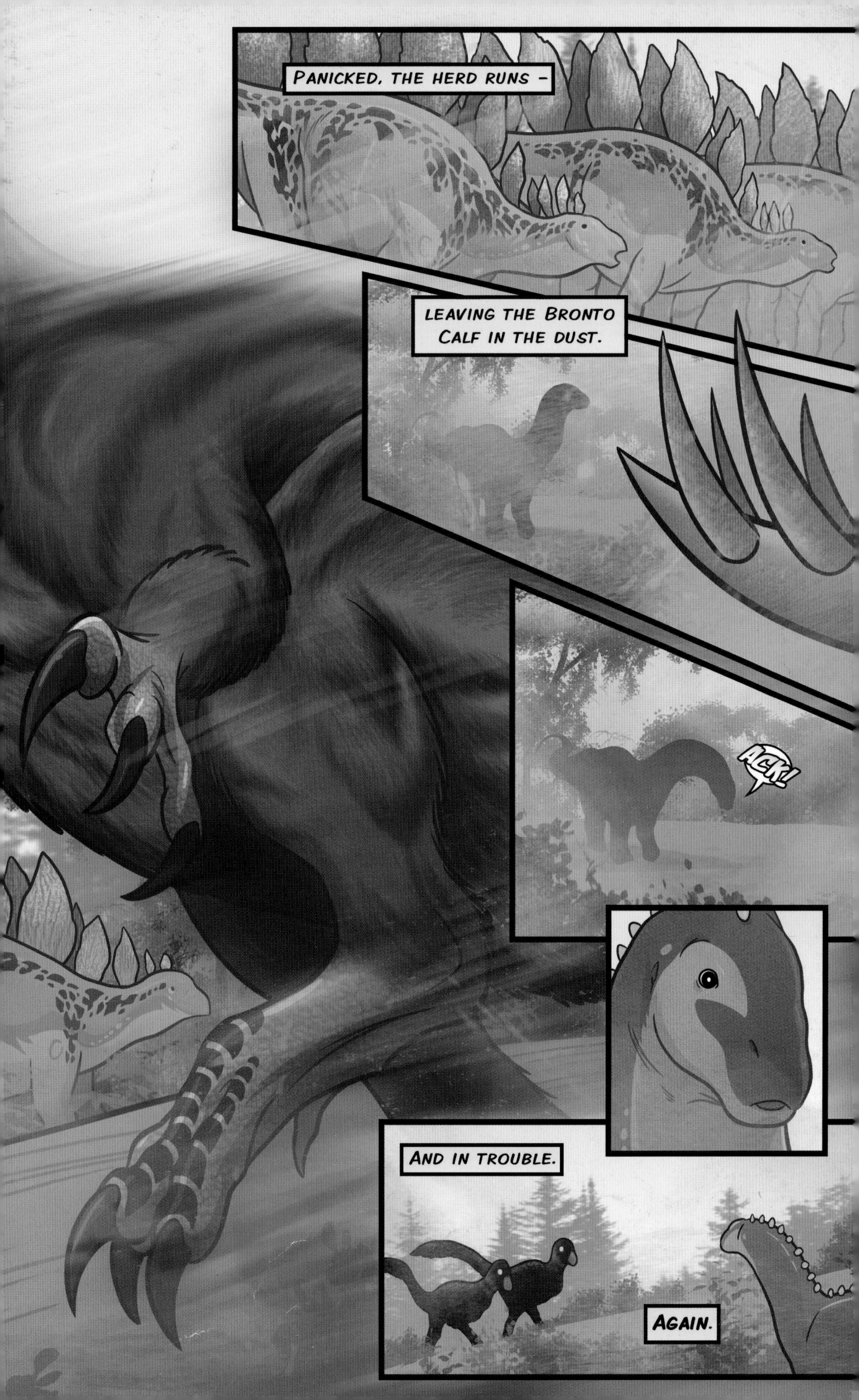
PANICKED, THE HERD RUNS –
LEAVING THE BRONTO CALF IN THE DUST.
ACK!
AND IN TROUBLE.
AGAIN.

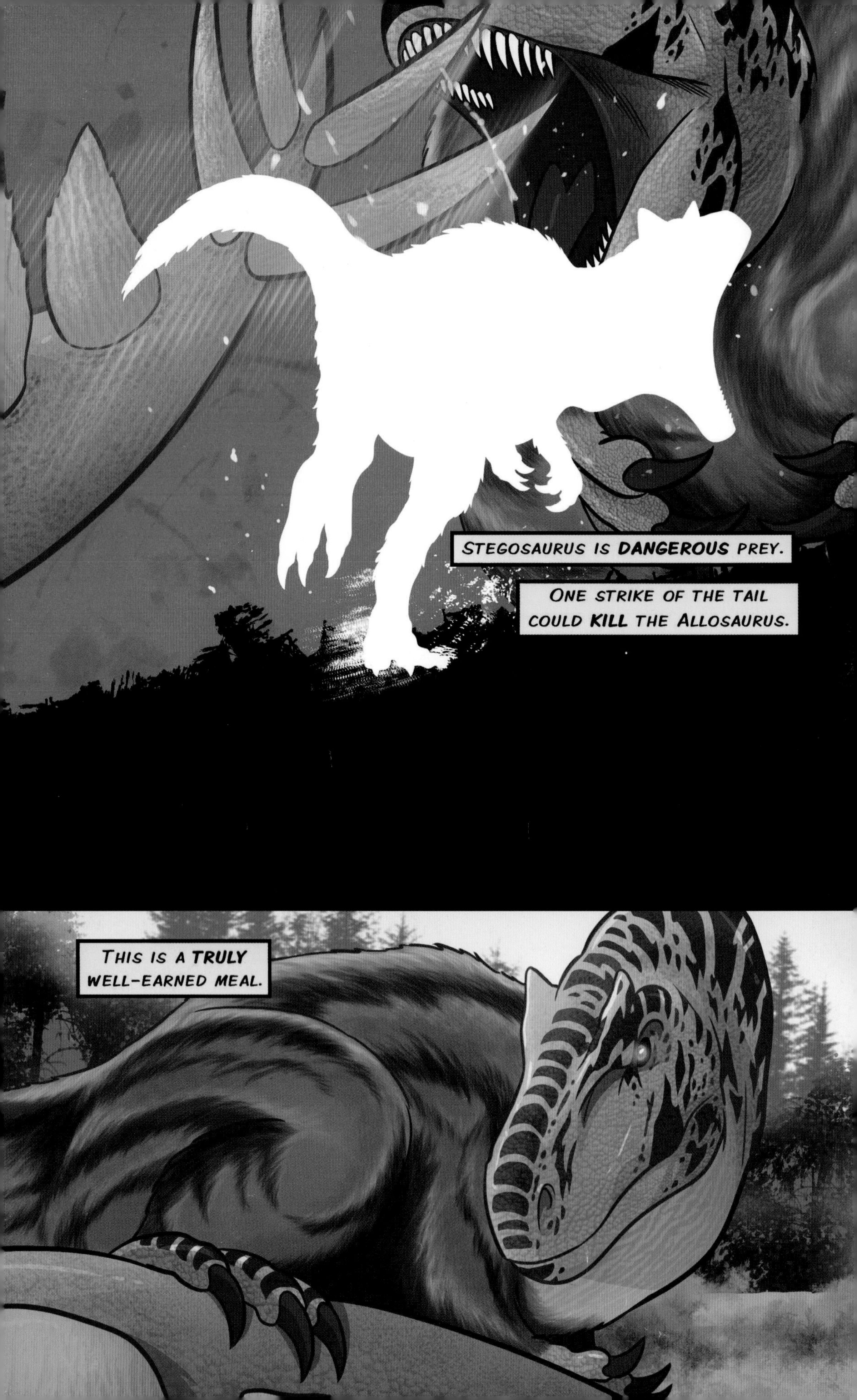
STEGOSAURUS IS **DANGEROUS** PREY.
ONE STRIKE OF THE TAIL COULD **KILL** THE ALLOSAURUS.
THIS IS A **TRULY** WELL-EARNED MEAL.

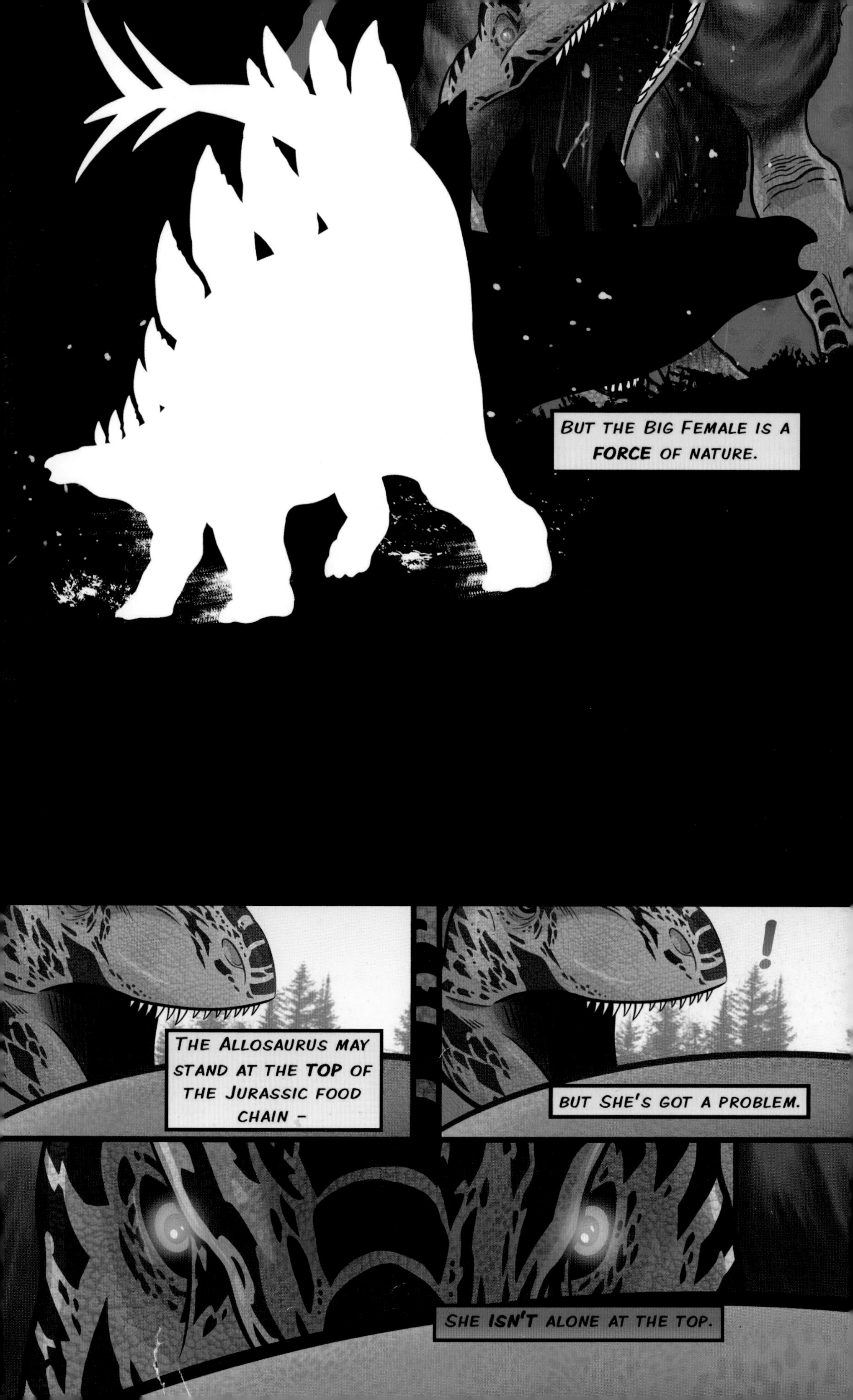
BUT THE BIG FEMALE IS A FORCE OF NATURE.
THE ALLOSAURUS MAY STAND AT THE TOP OF THE JURASSIC FOOD CHAIN –
!
BUT SHE'S GOT A PROBLEM.
SHE ISN'T ALONE AT THE TOP.

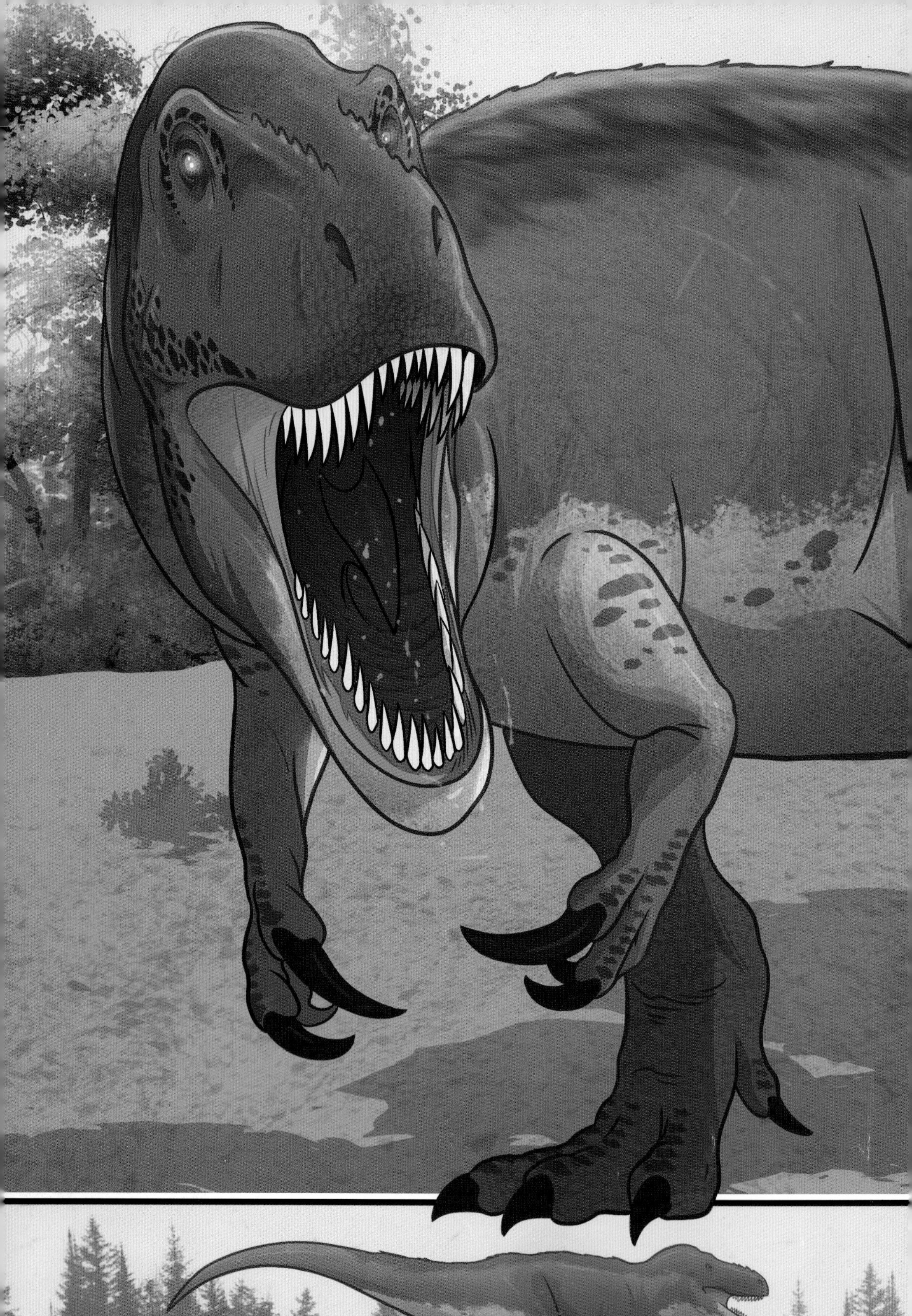
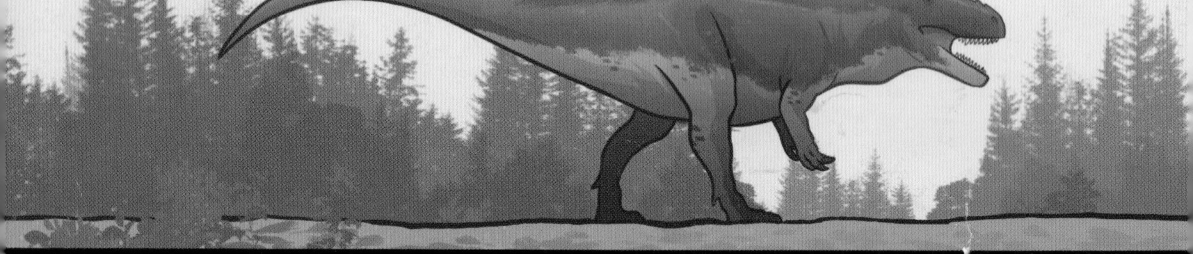

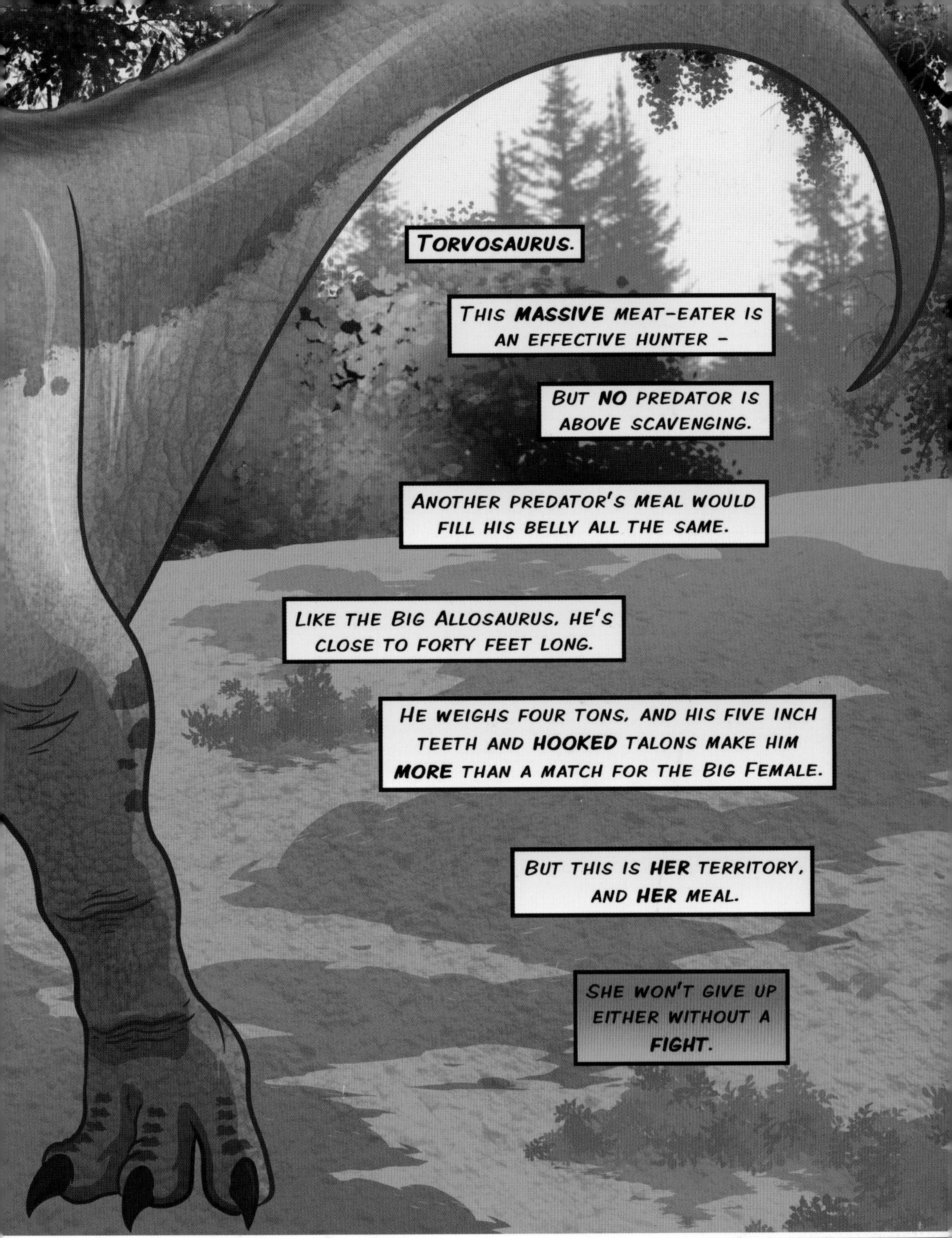
TORVOSAURUS.
THIS MASSIVE MEAT-EATER IS AN EFFECTIVE HUNTER –
BUT NO PREDATOR IS ABOVE SCAVENGING.
ANOTHER PREDATOR'S MEAL WOULD FILL HIS BELLY ALL THE SAME.
LIKE THE BIG ALLOSAURUS, HE'S CLOSE TO FORTY FEET LONG.
HE WEIGHS FOUR TONS, AND HIS FIVE INCH TEETH AND HOOKED TALONS MAKE HIM MORE THAN A MATCH FOR THE BIG FEMALE.
BUT THIS IS HER TERRITORY, AND HER MEAL.
SHE WON'T GIVE UP EITHER WITHOUT A FIGHT.
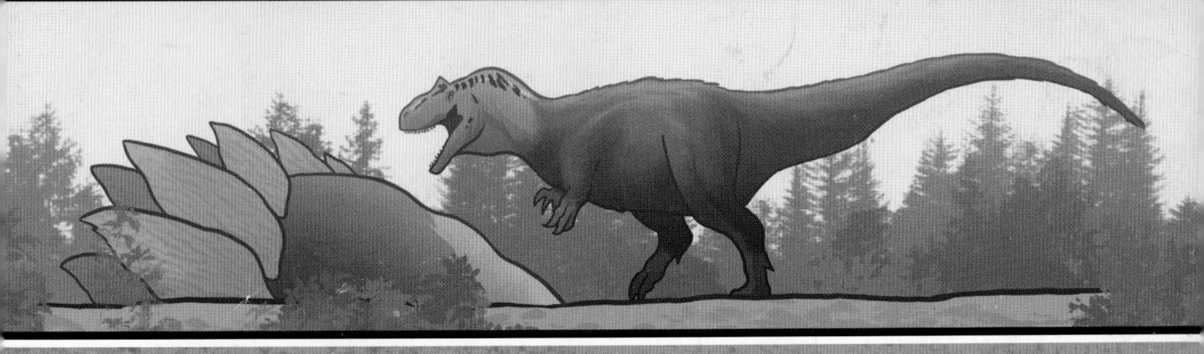

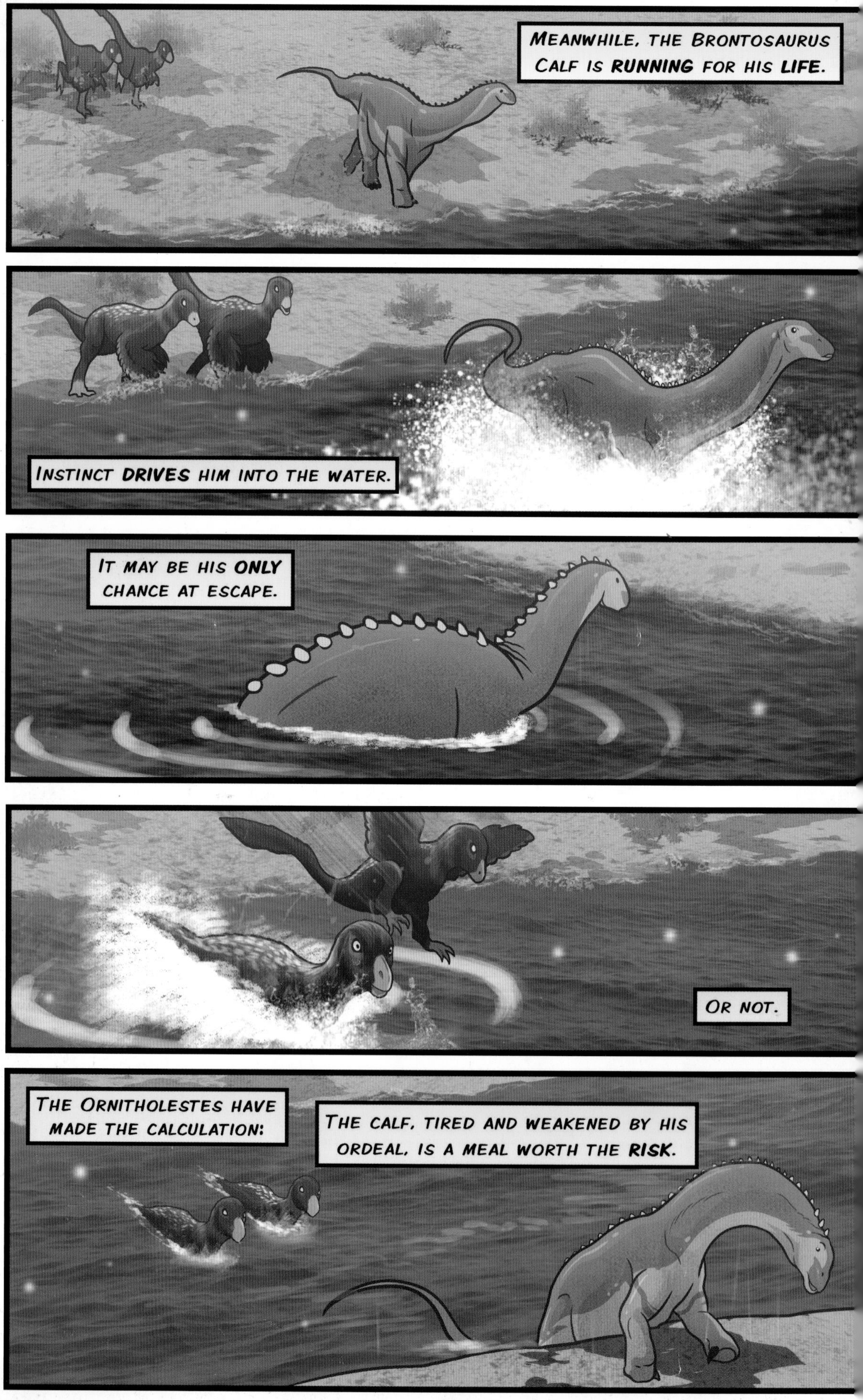
MEANWHILE, THE BRONTOSAURUS CALF IS RUNNING FOR HIS LIFE.
INSTINCT DRIVES HIM INTO THE WATER.
IT MAY BE HIS ONLY CHANCE AT ESCAPE.
OR NOT.
THE ORNITHOLESTES HAVE MADE THE CALCULATION:
THE CALF, TIRED AND WEAKENED BY HIS ORDEAL, IS A MEAL WORTH THE RISK.

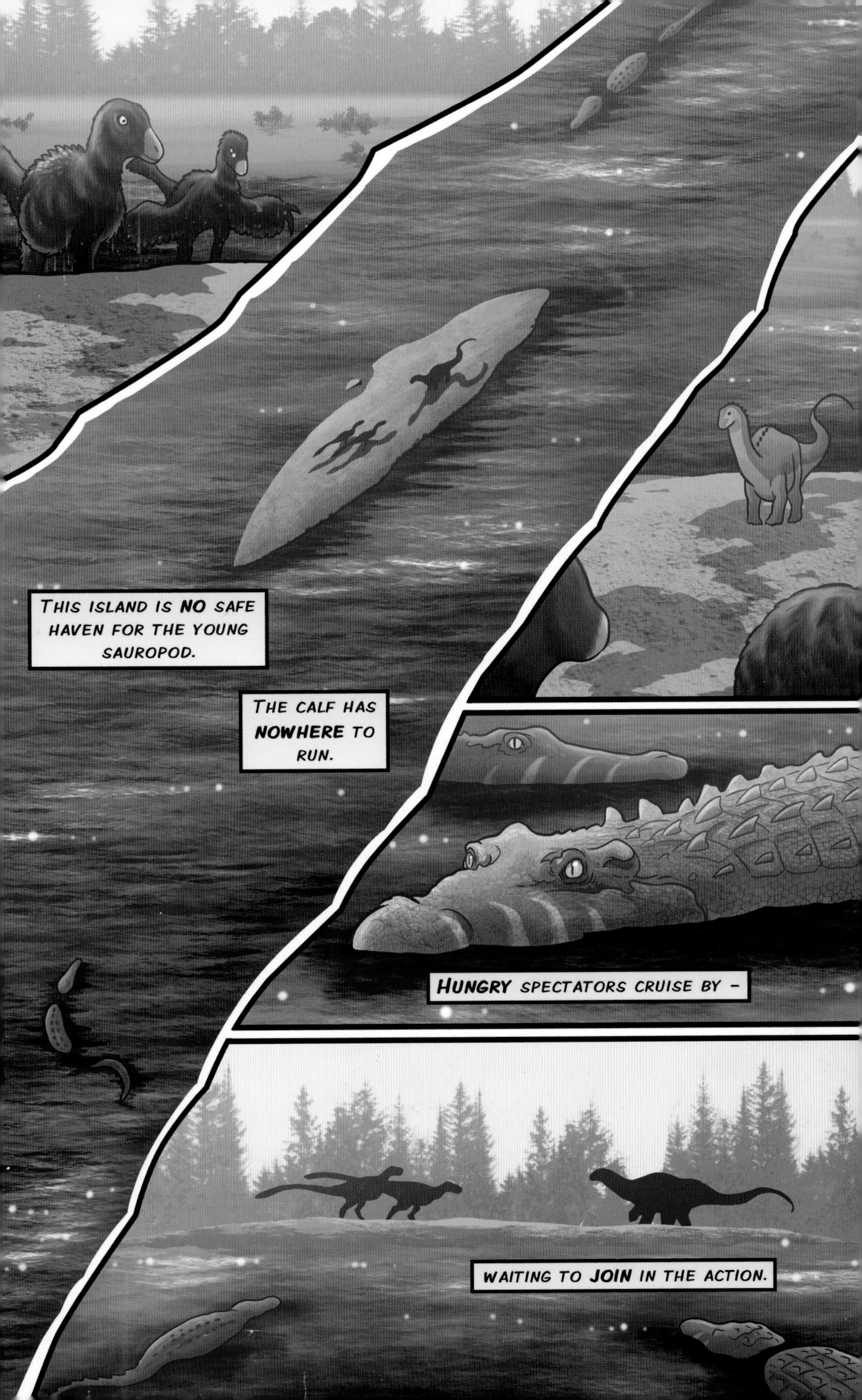
THIS ISLAND IS **NO** SAFE HAVEN FOR THE YOUNG SAUROPOD.
THE CALF HAS **NOWHERE** TO RUN.
HUNGRY SPECTATORS CRUISE BY –
WAITING TO **JOIN** IN THE ACTION.

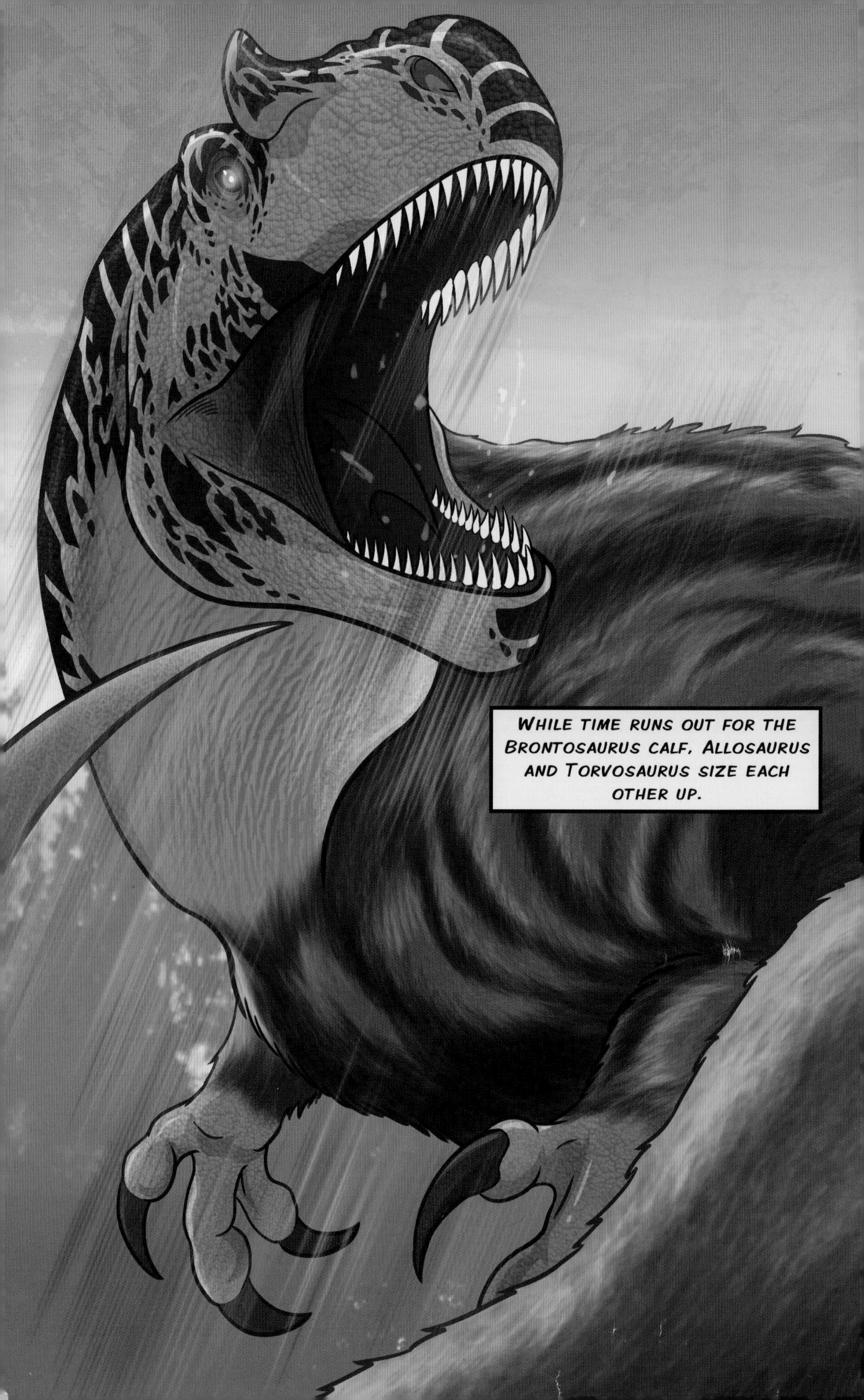
WHILE TIME RUNS OUT FOR THE BRONTOSAURUS CALF, ALLOSAURUS AND TORVOSAURUS SIZE EACH OTHER UP.

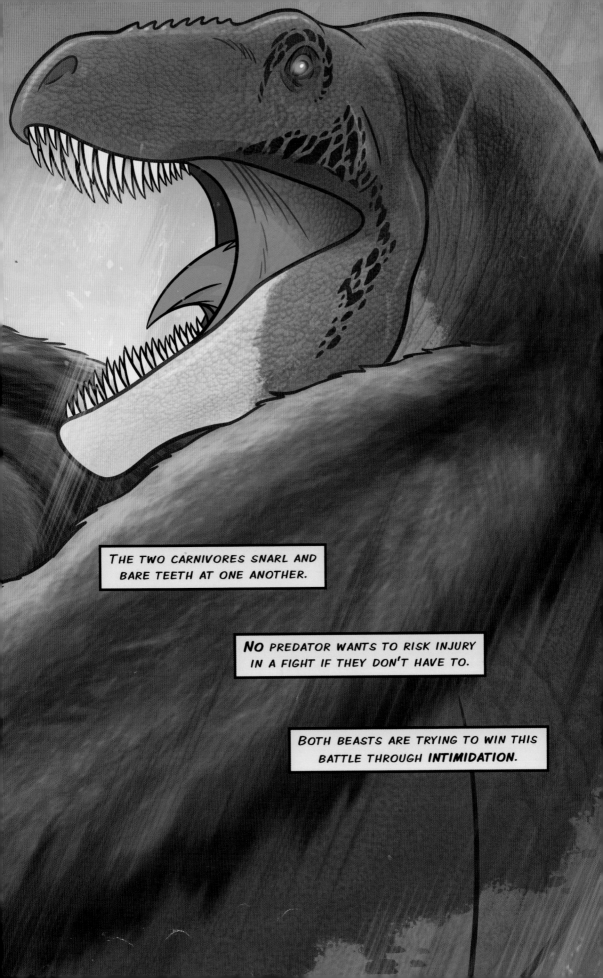

The two carnivores snarl and bare teeth at one another.

No predator wants to risk injury in a fight if they don't have to.

Both beasts are trying to win this battle through INTIMIDATION.

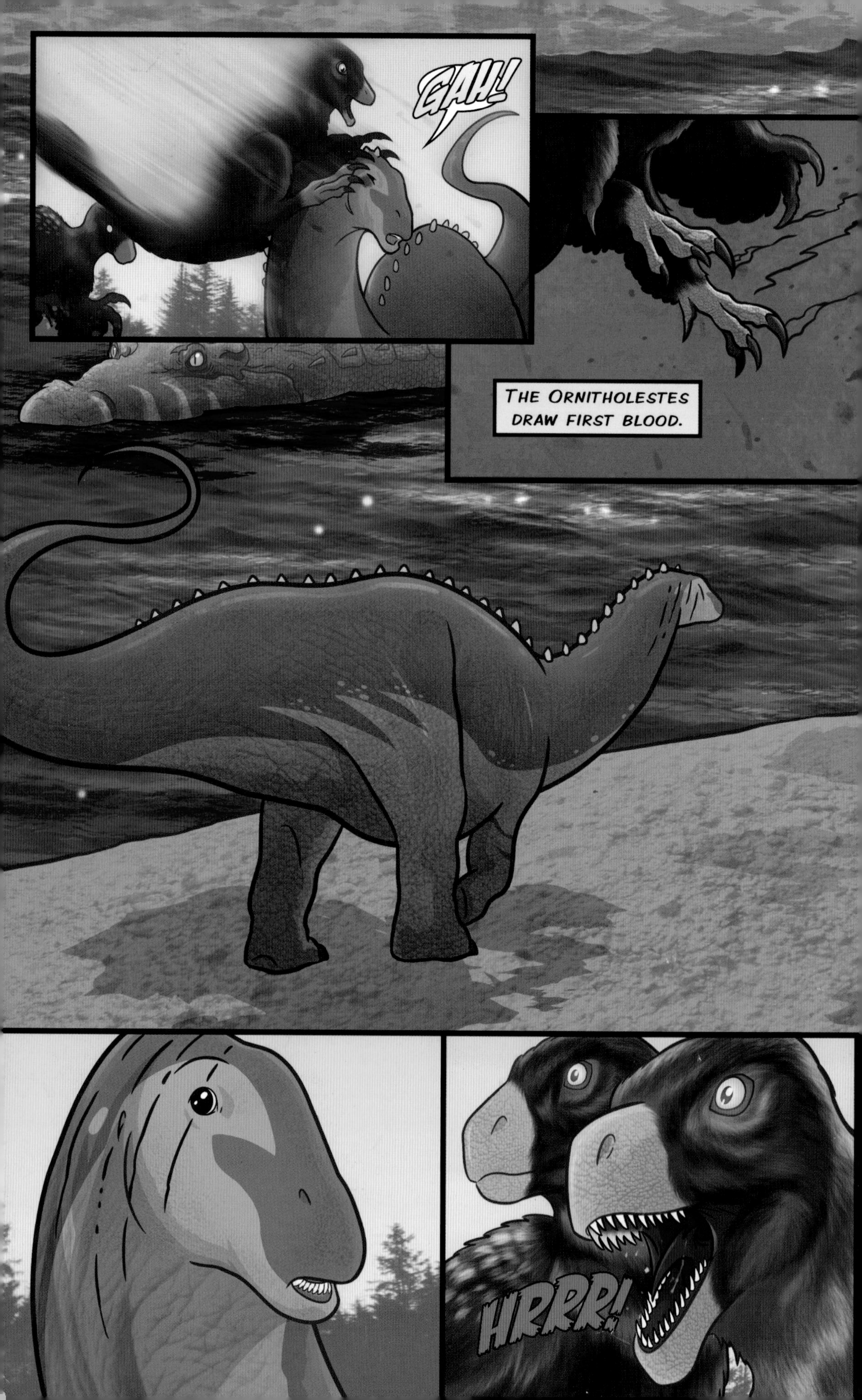
GAH!
THE ORNITHOLESTES DRAW FIRST BLOOD.
HRRR!

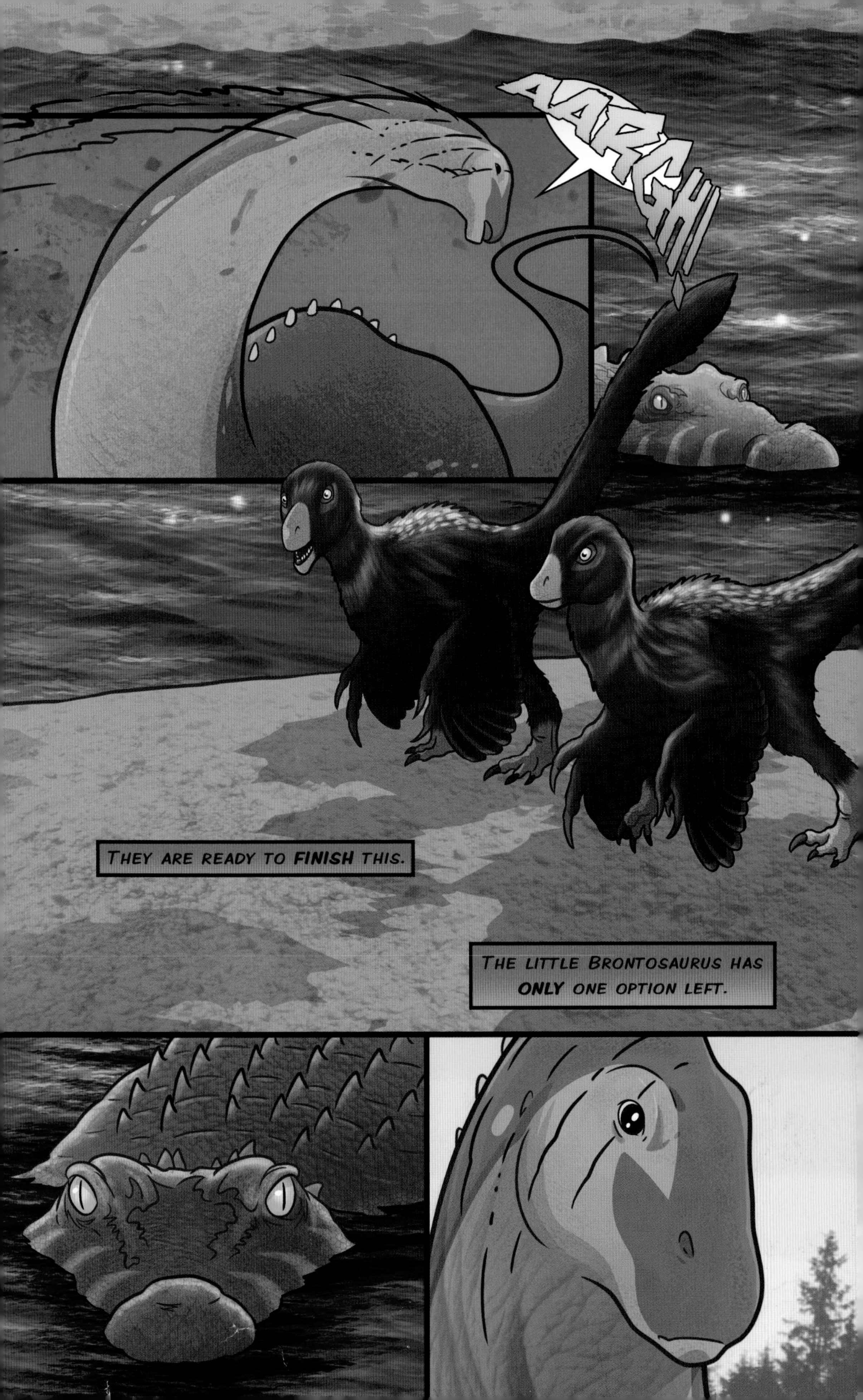
AARGH!!
THEY ARE READY TO FINISH THIS.
THE LITTLE BRONTOSAURUS HAS ONLY ONE OPTION LEFT.

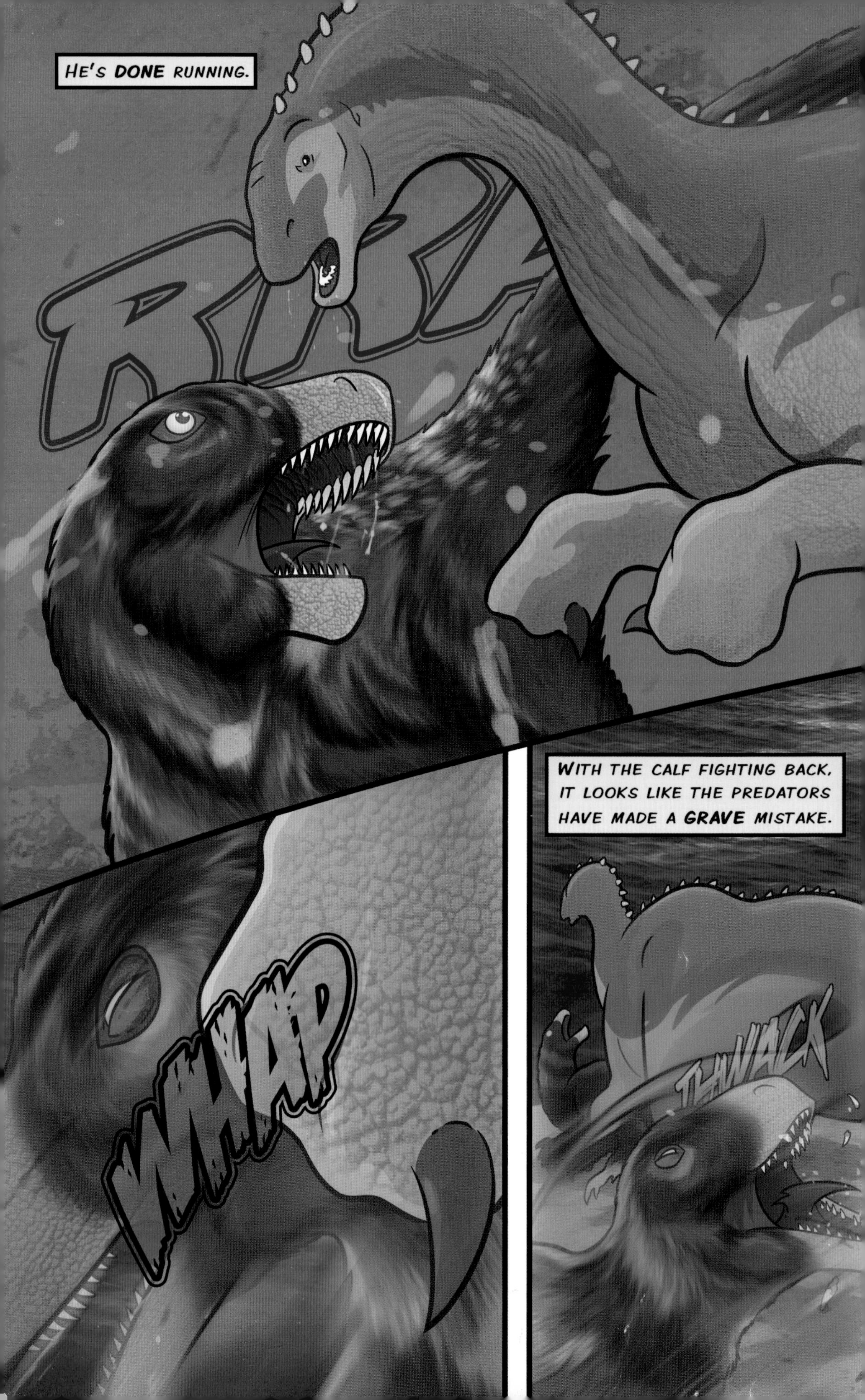
HE'S DONE RUNNING.
WHAP
WITH THE CALF FIGHTING BACK, IT LOOKS LIKE THE PREDATORS HAVE MADE A GRAVE MISTAKE.
THWACK

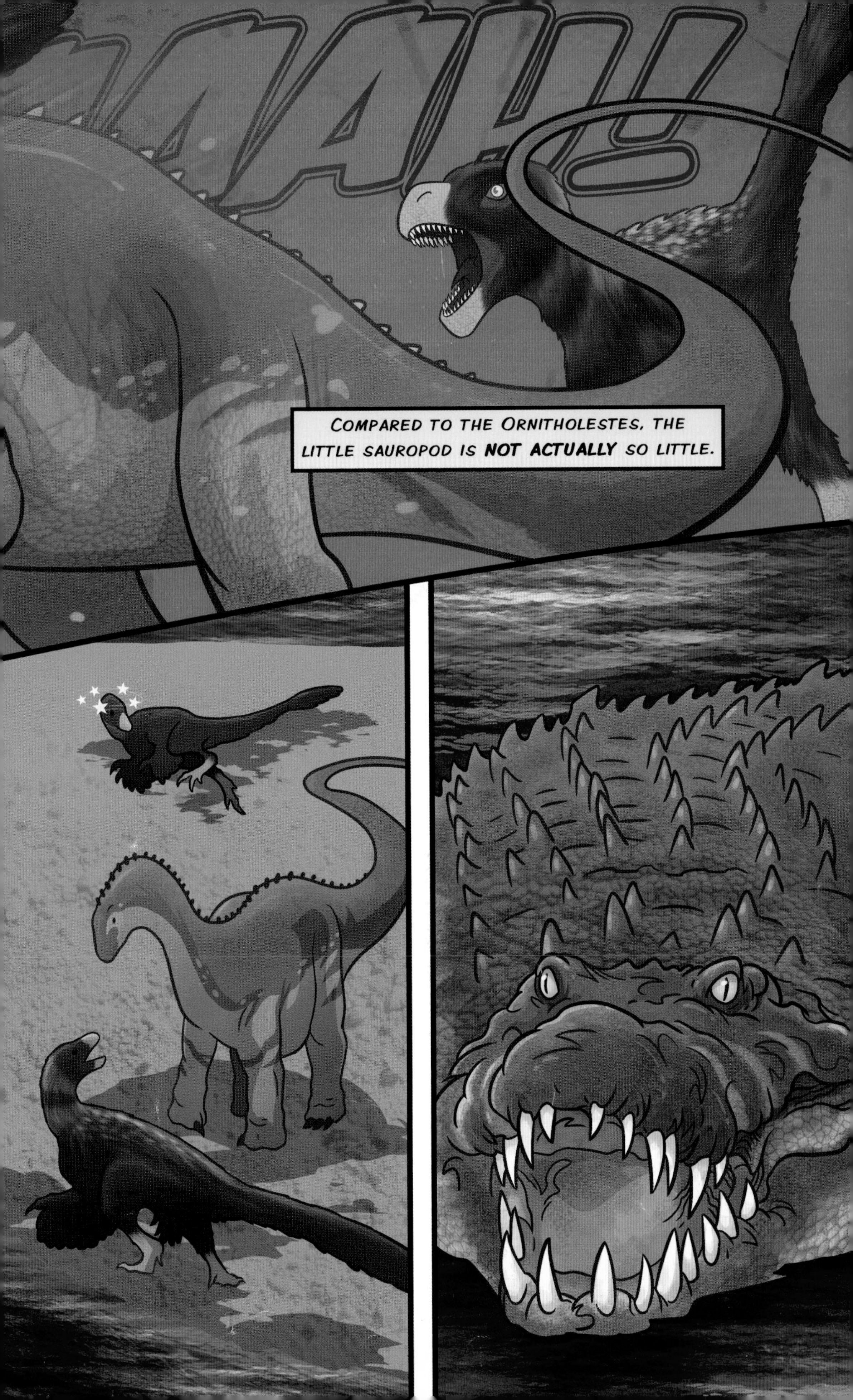
COMPARED TO THE ORNITHOLESTES, THE LITTLE SAUROPOD IS **NOT ACTUALLY** SO LITTLE.

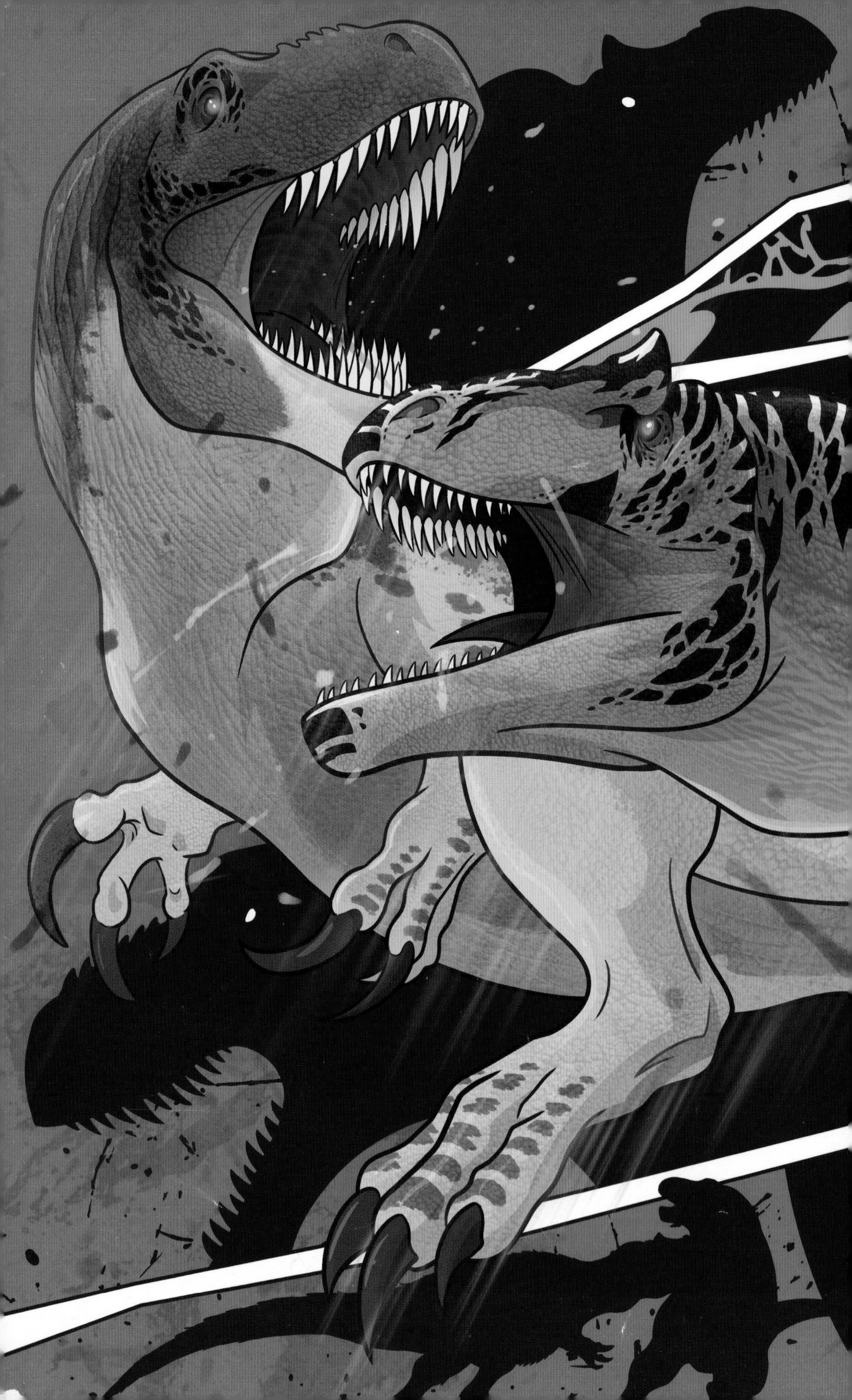

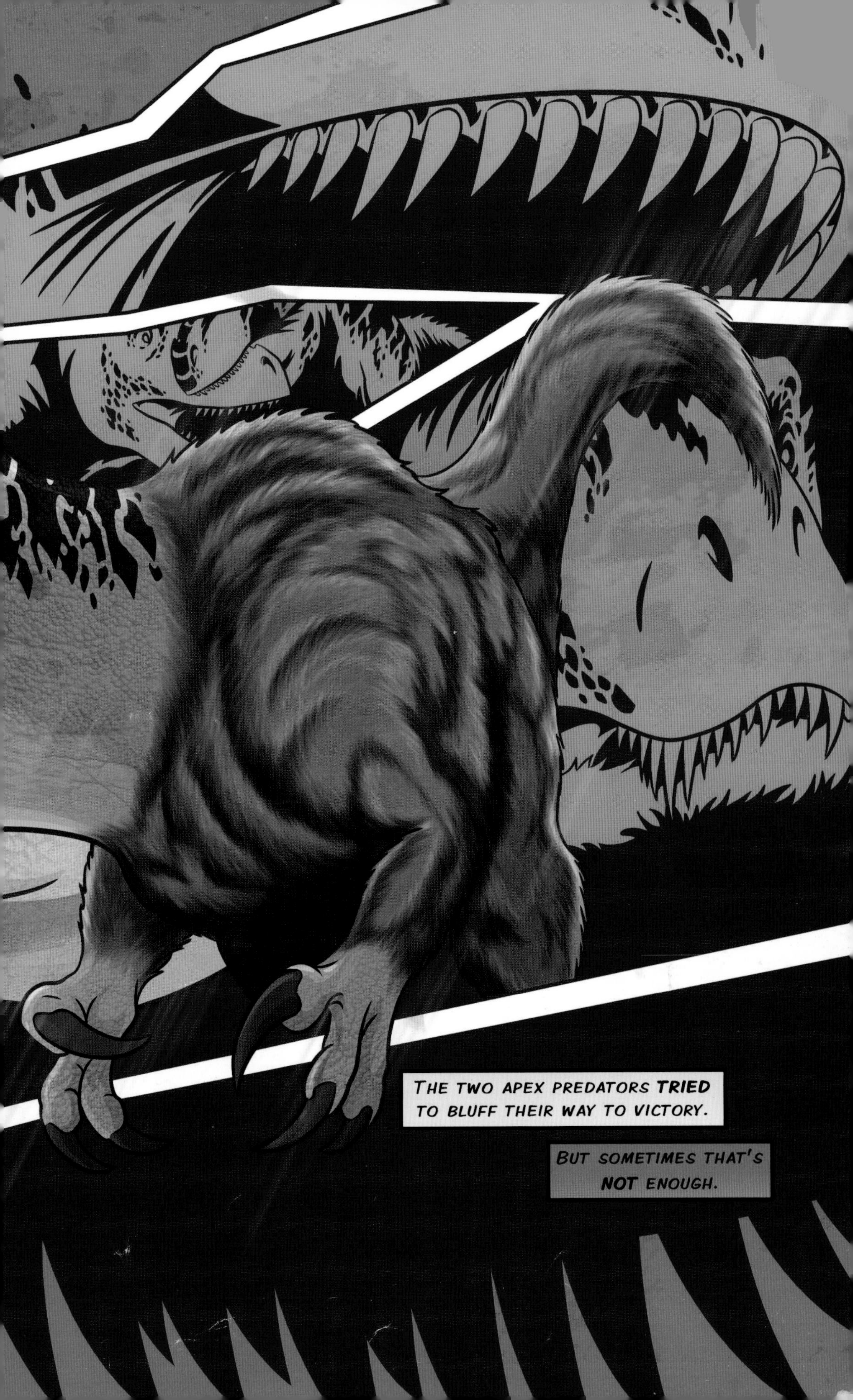
THE TWO APEX PREDATORS **TRIED** TO BLUFF THEIR WAY TO VICTORY.
BUT SOMETIMES THAT'S **NOT** ENOUGH.

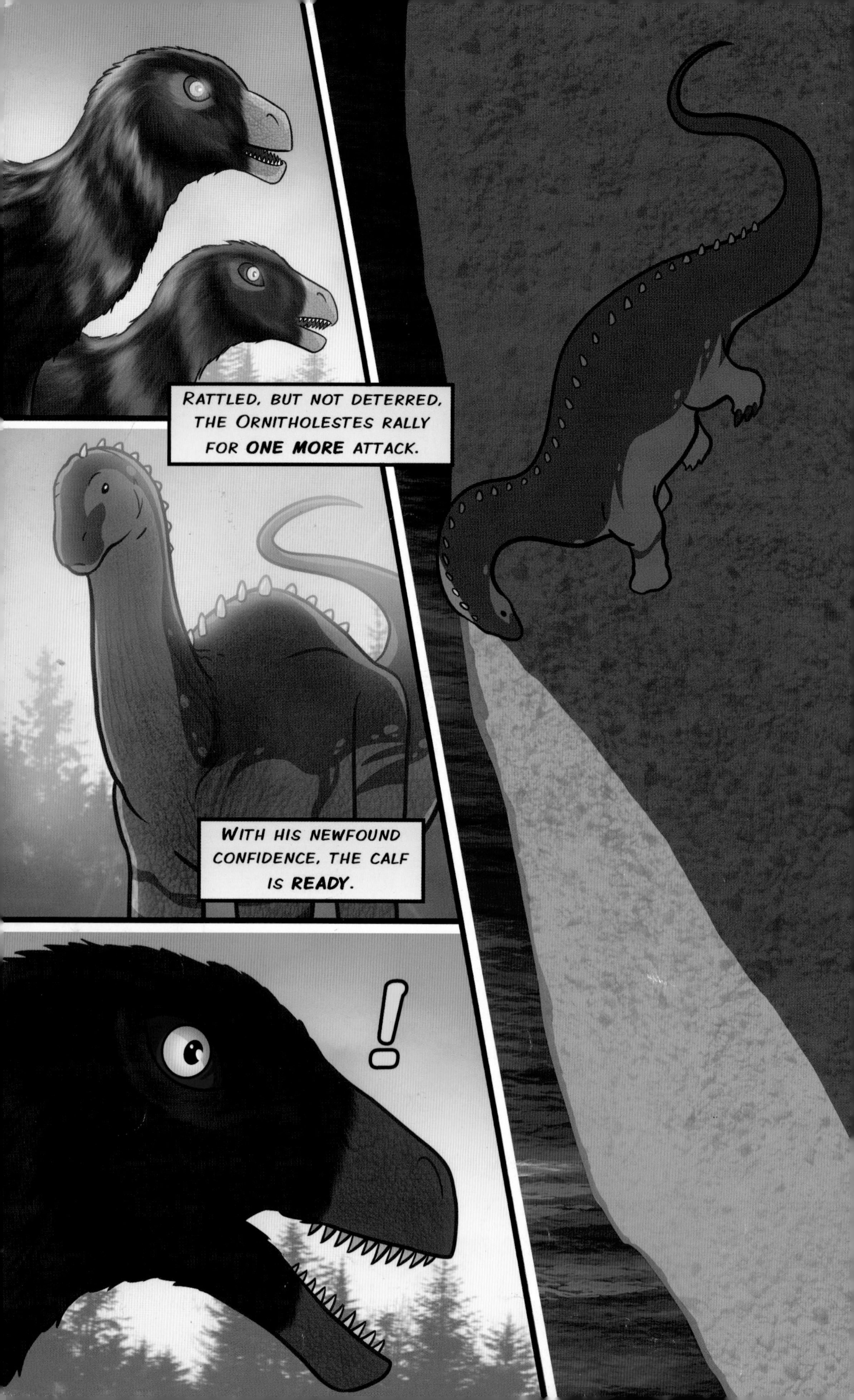
RATTLED, BUT NOT DETERRED, THE ORNITHOLESTES RALLY FOR ONE MORE ATTACK.
WITH HIS NEWFOUND CONFIDENCE, THE CALF IS READY.
!

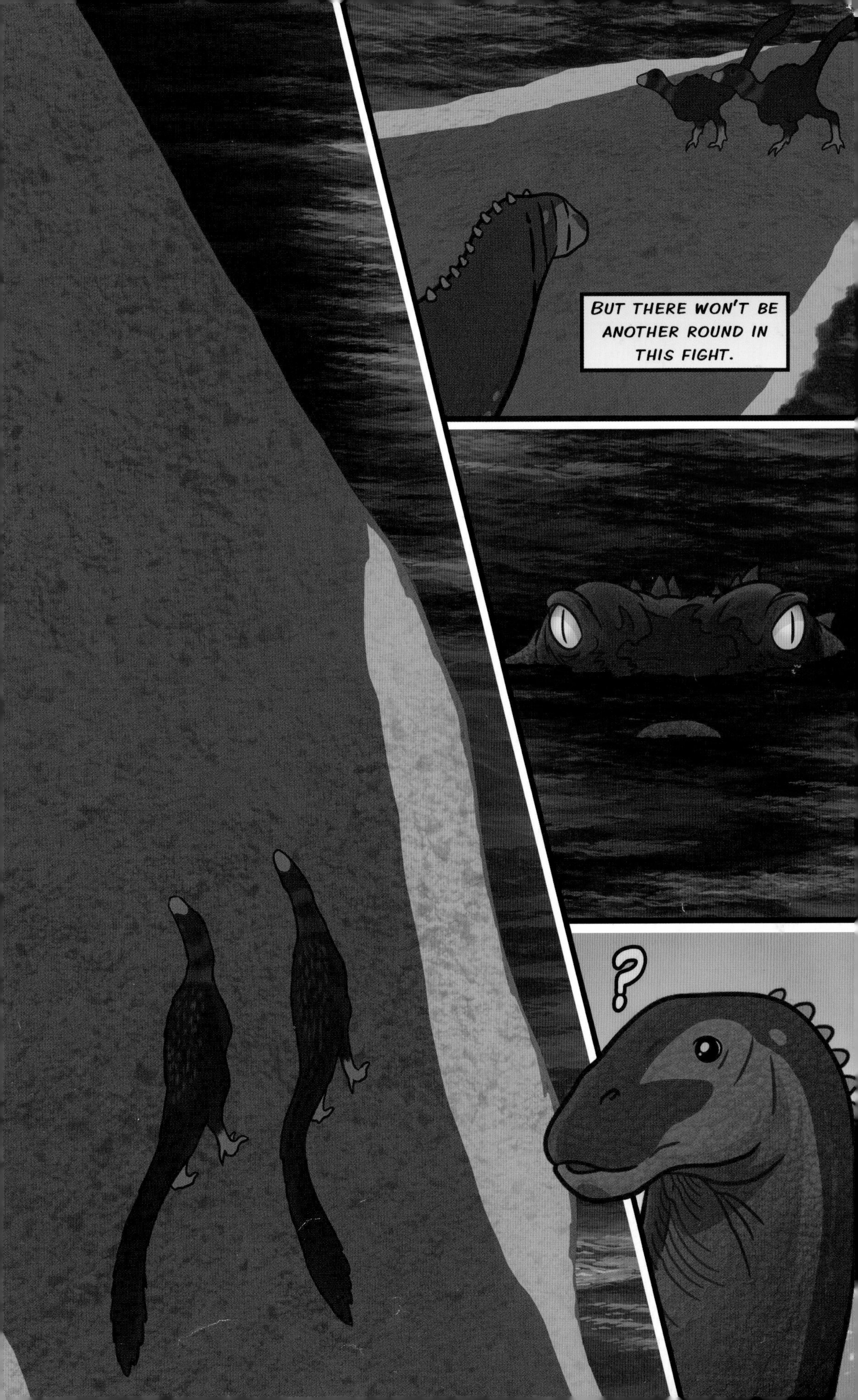
BUT THERE WON'T BE ANOTHER ROUND IN THIS FIGHT.
?

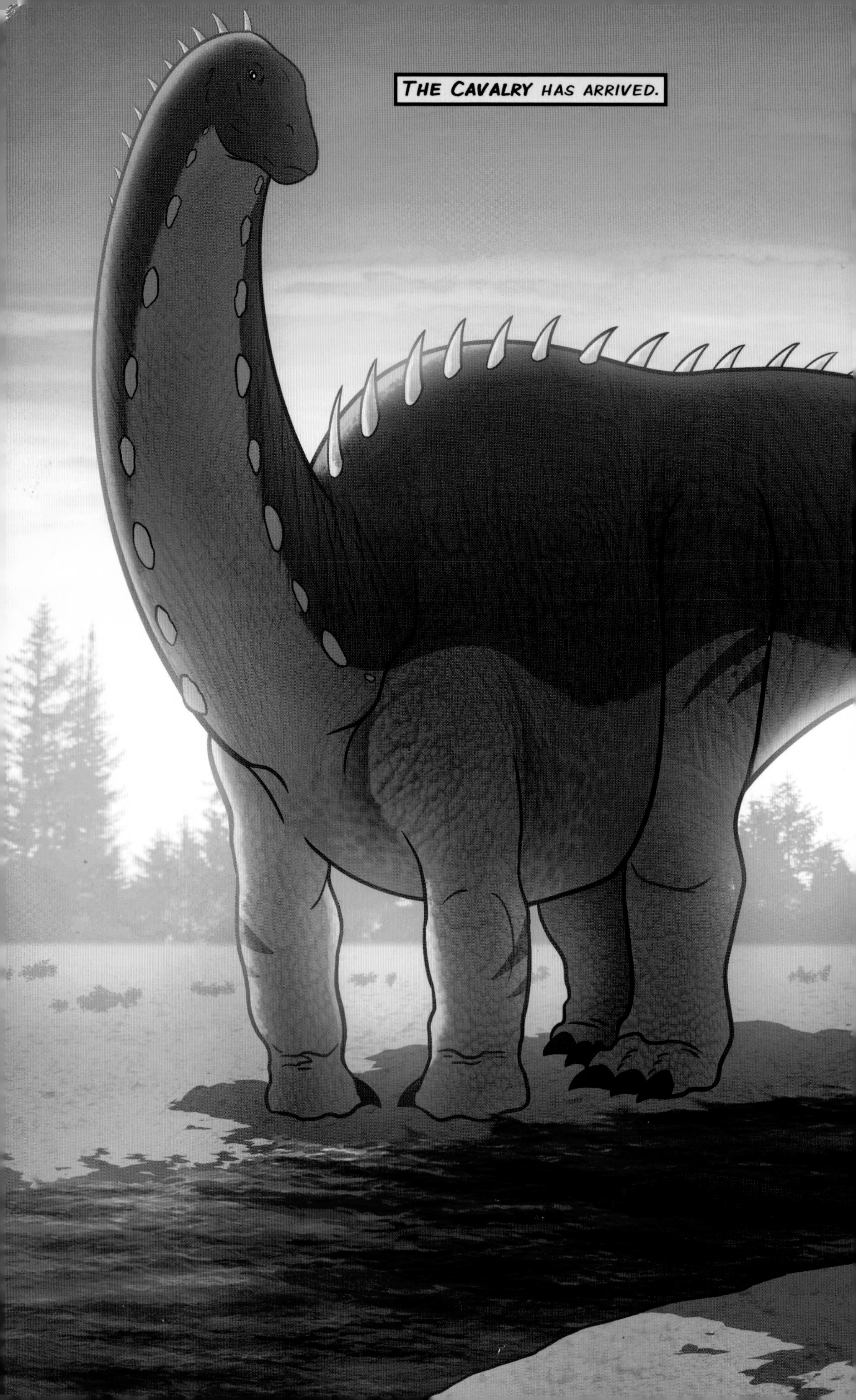
THE CAVALRY HAS ARRIVED.

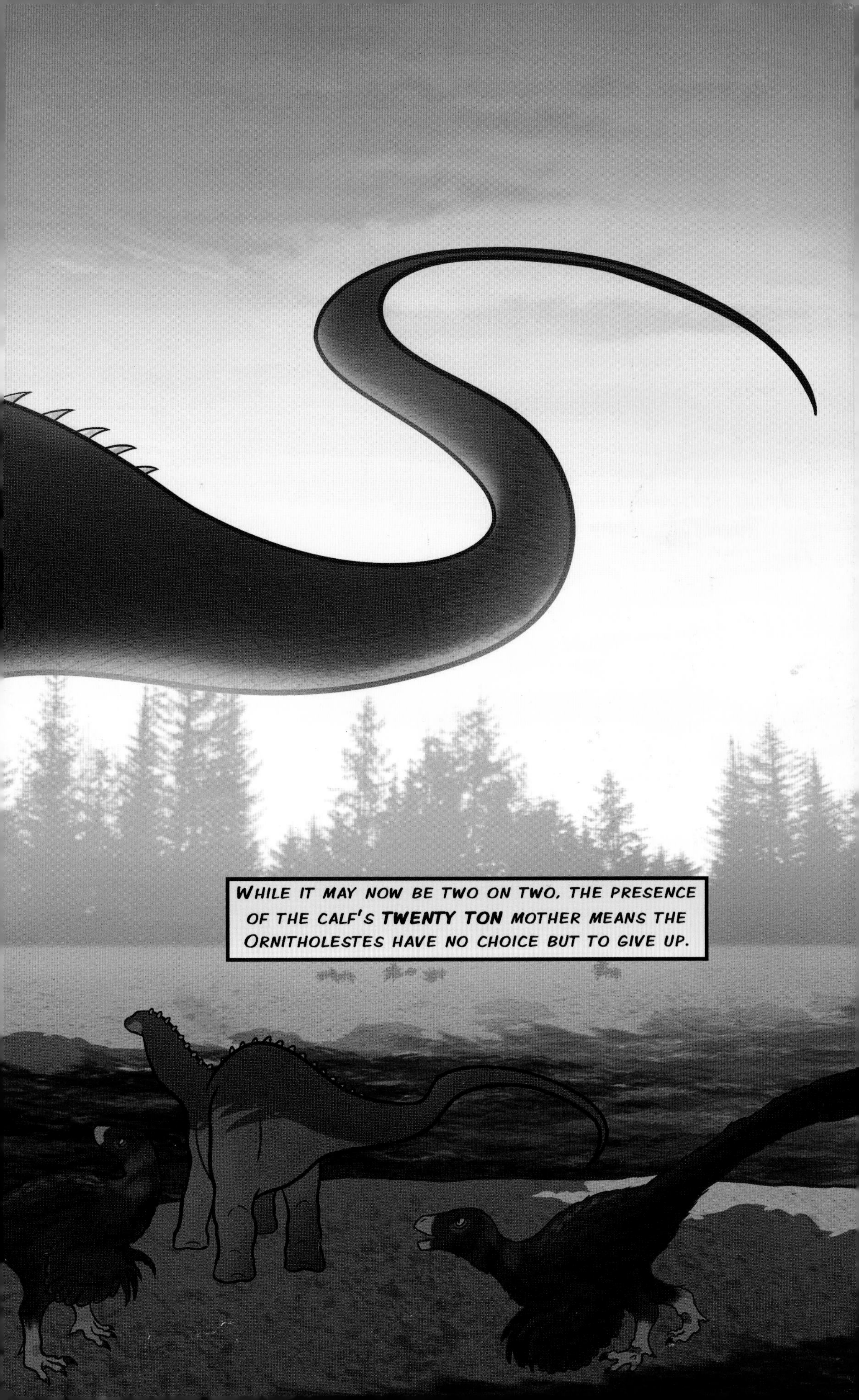
WHILE IT MAY NOW BE TWO ON TWO, THE PRESENCE OF THE CALF'S TWENTY TON MOTHER MEANS THE ORNITHOLESTES HAVE NO CHOICE BUT TO GIVE UP.

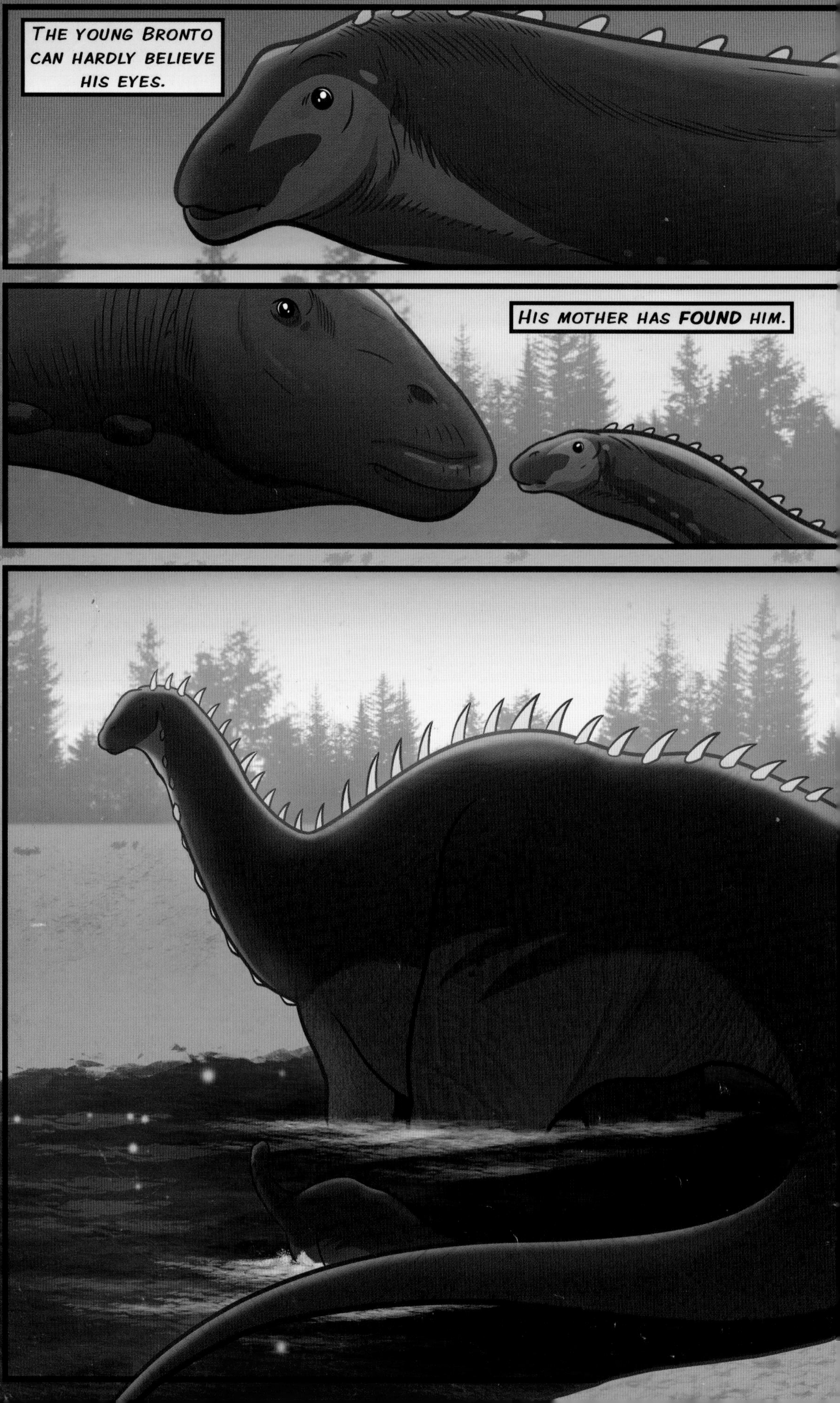
THE YOUNG BRONTO CAN HARDLY BELIEVE HIS EYES.
HIS MOTHER HAS FOUND HIM.

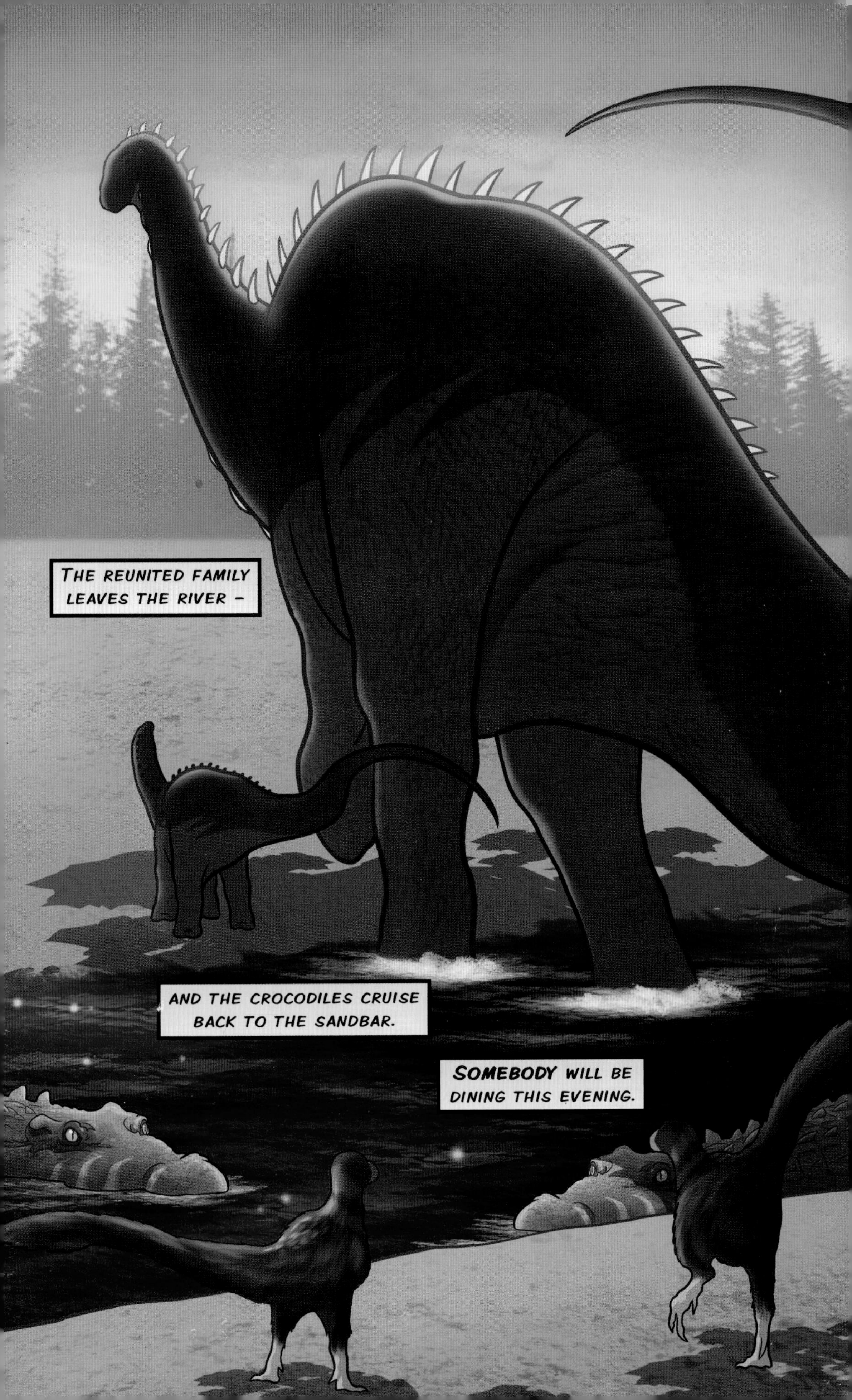
THE REUNITED FAMILY LEAVES THE RIVER –
AND THE CROCODILES CRUISE BACK TO THE SANDBAR.
SOMEBODY WILL BE DINING THIS EVENING.

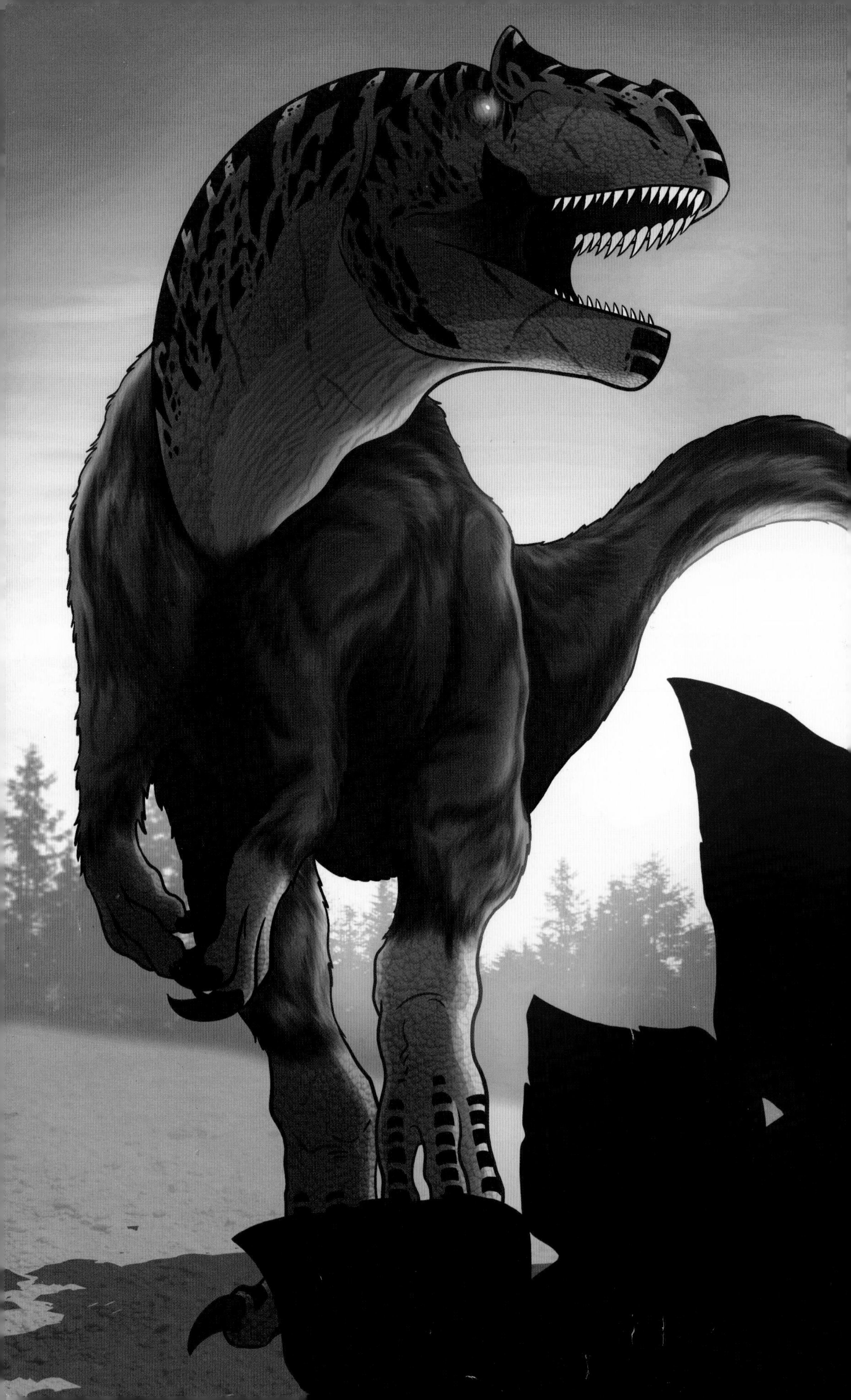

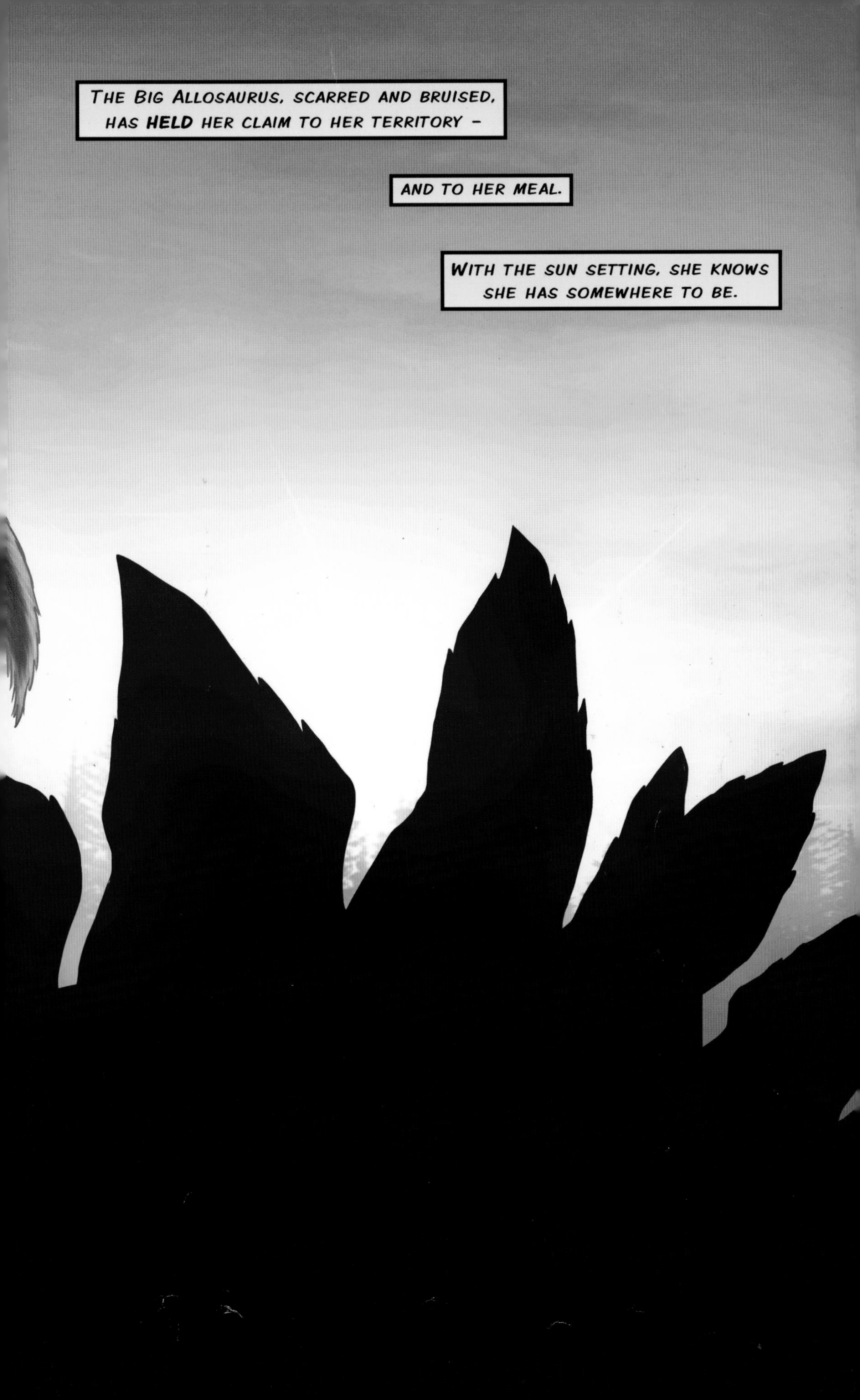
THE BIG ALLOSAURUS, SCARRED AND BRUISED, HAS **HELD** HER CLAIM TO HER TERRITORY –
AND TO HER MEAL.
WITH THE SUN SETTING, SHE KNOWS SHE HAS SOMEWHERE TO BE.

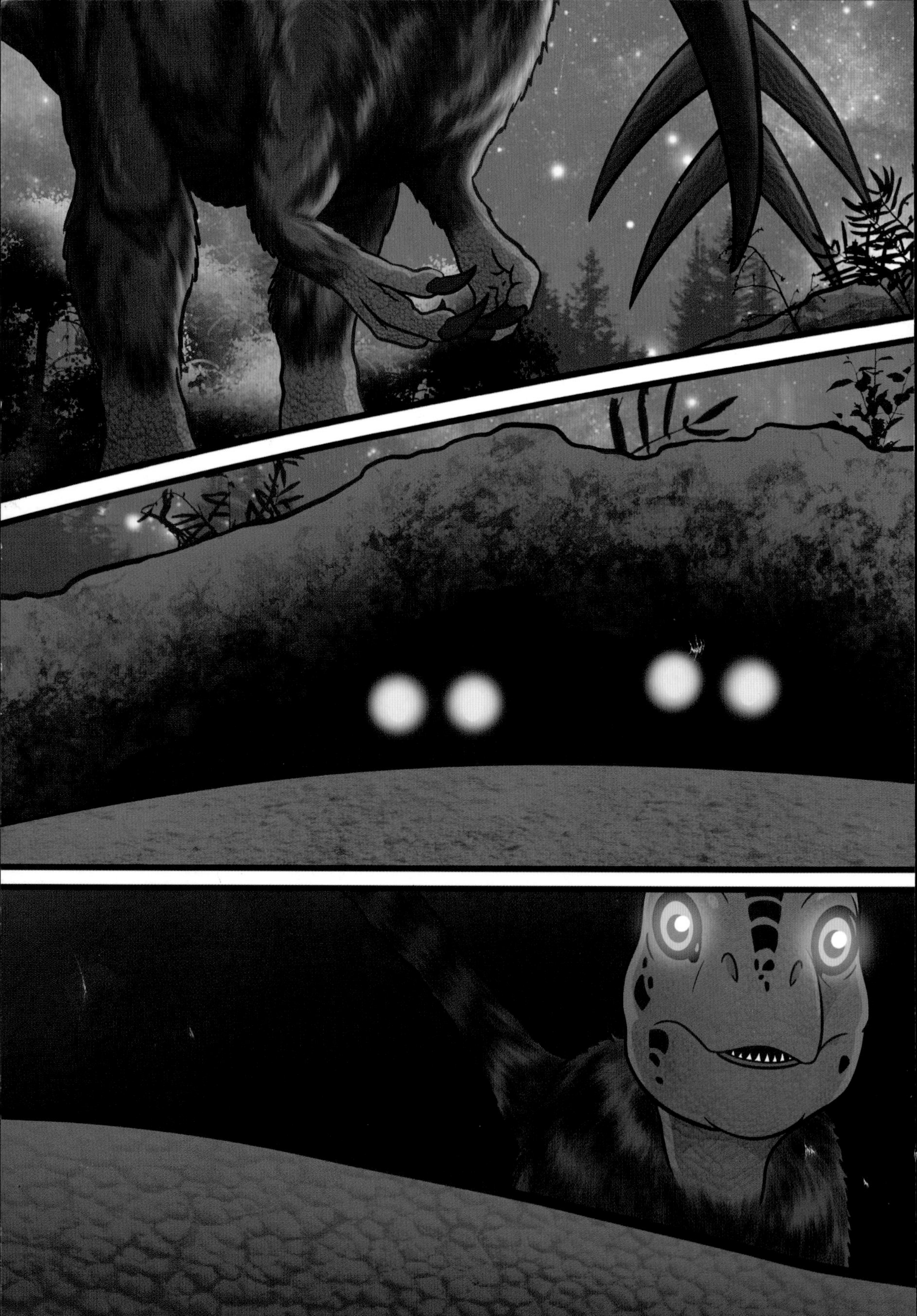

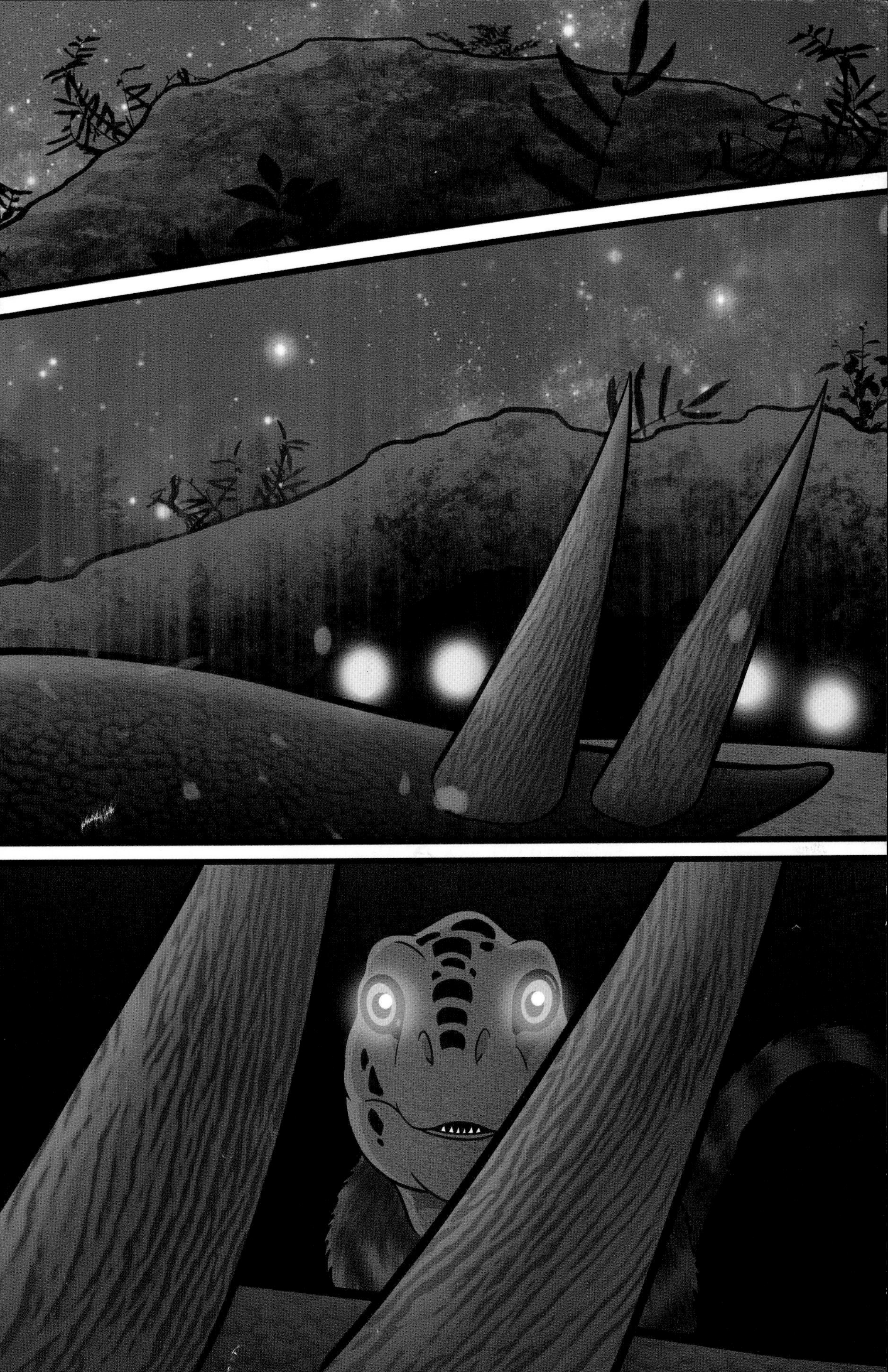

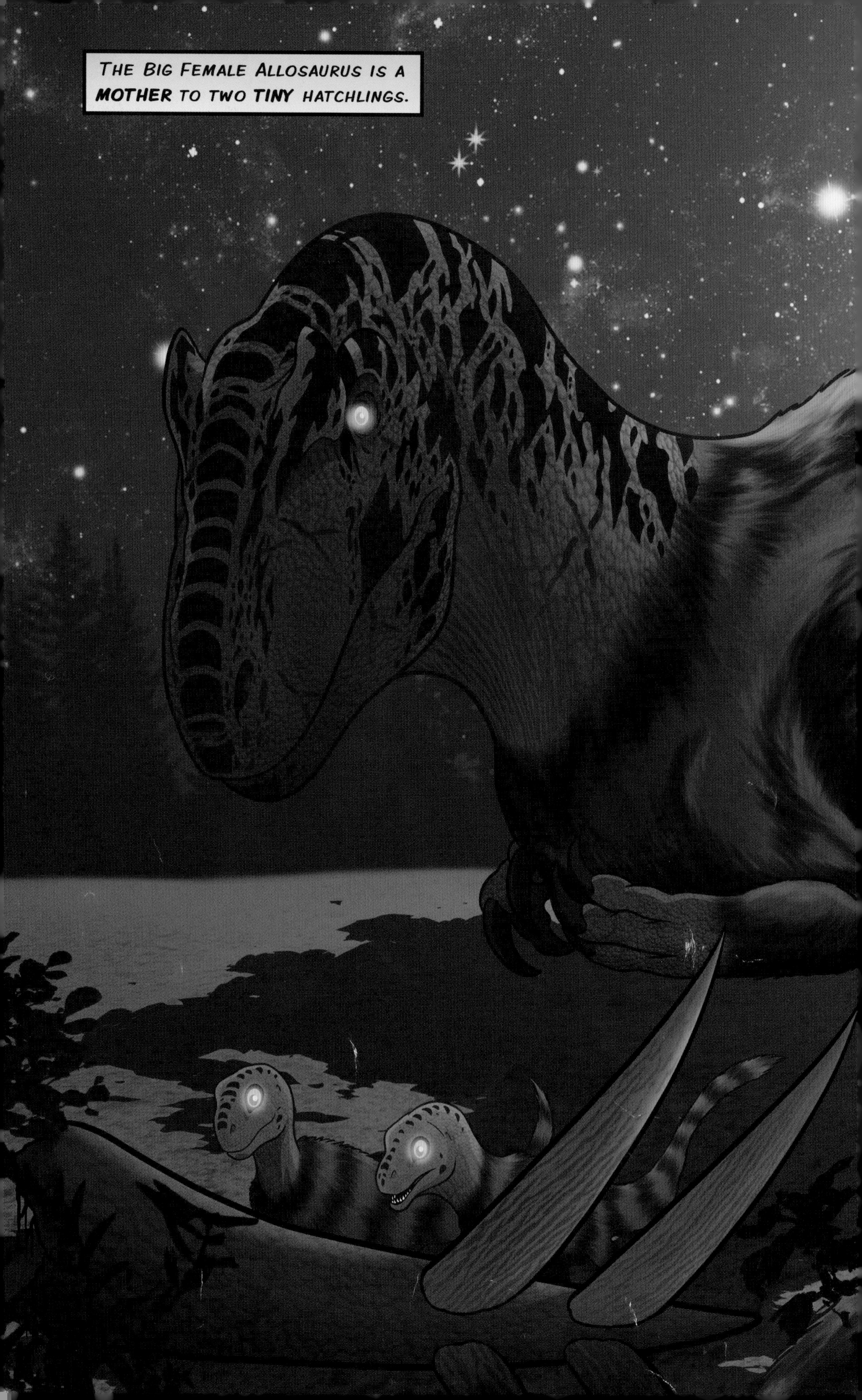
THE BIG FEMALE ALLOSAURUS IS A MOTHER TO TWO TINY HATCHLINGS.

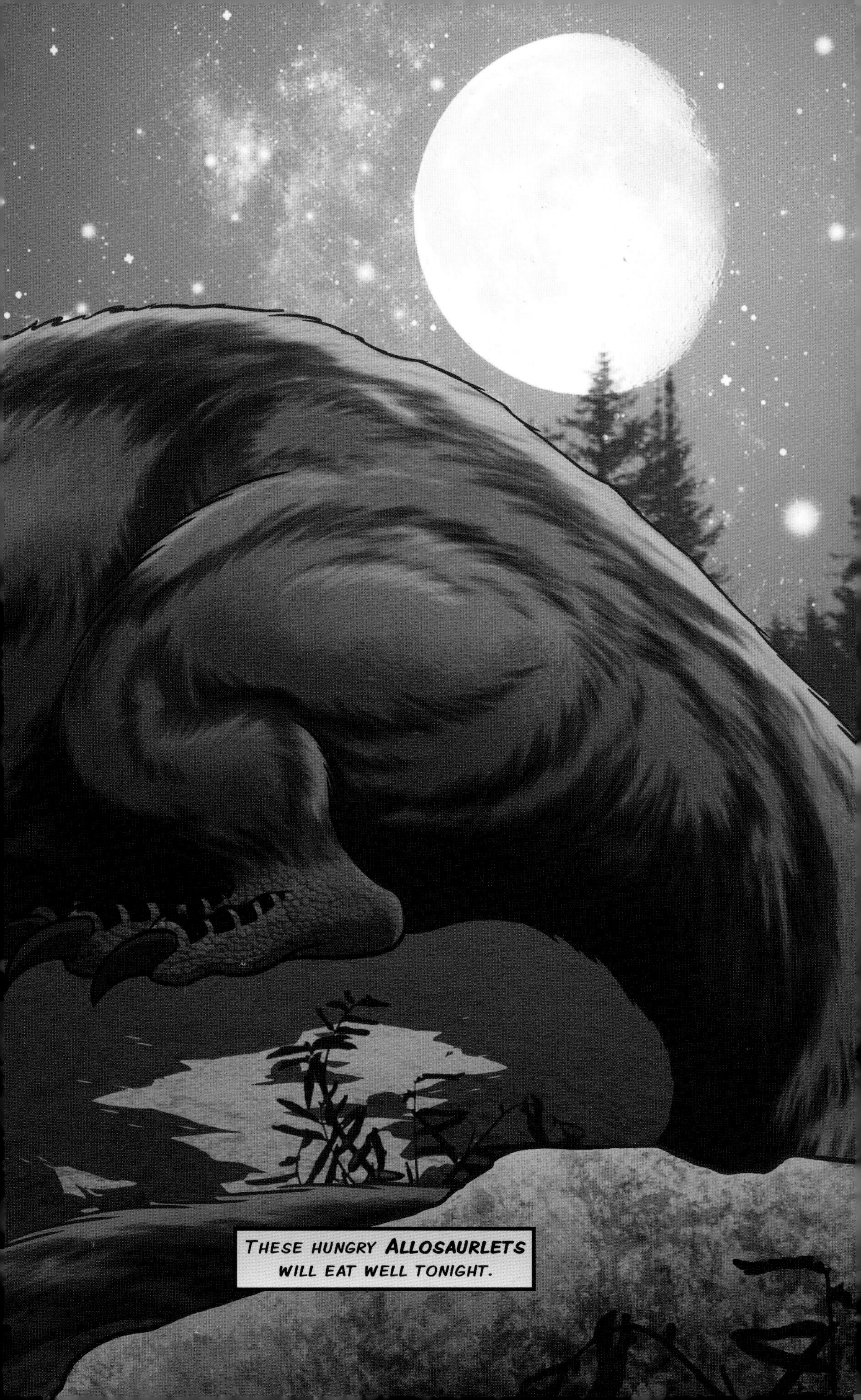
THESE HUNGRY ALLOSAURLETS WILL EAT WELL TONIGHT.

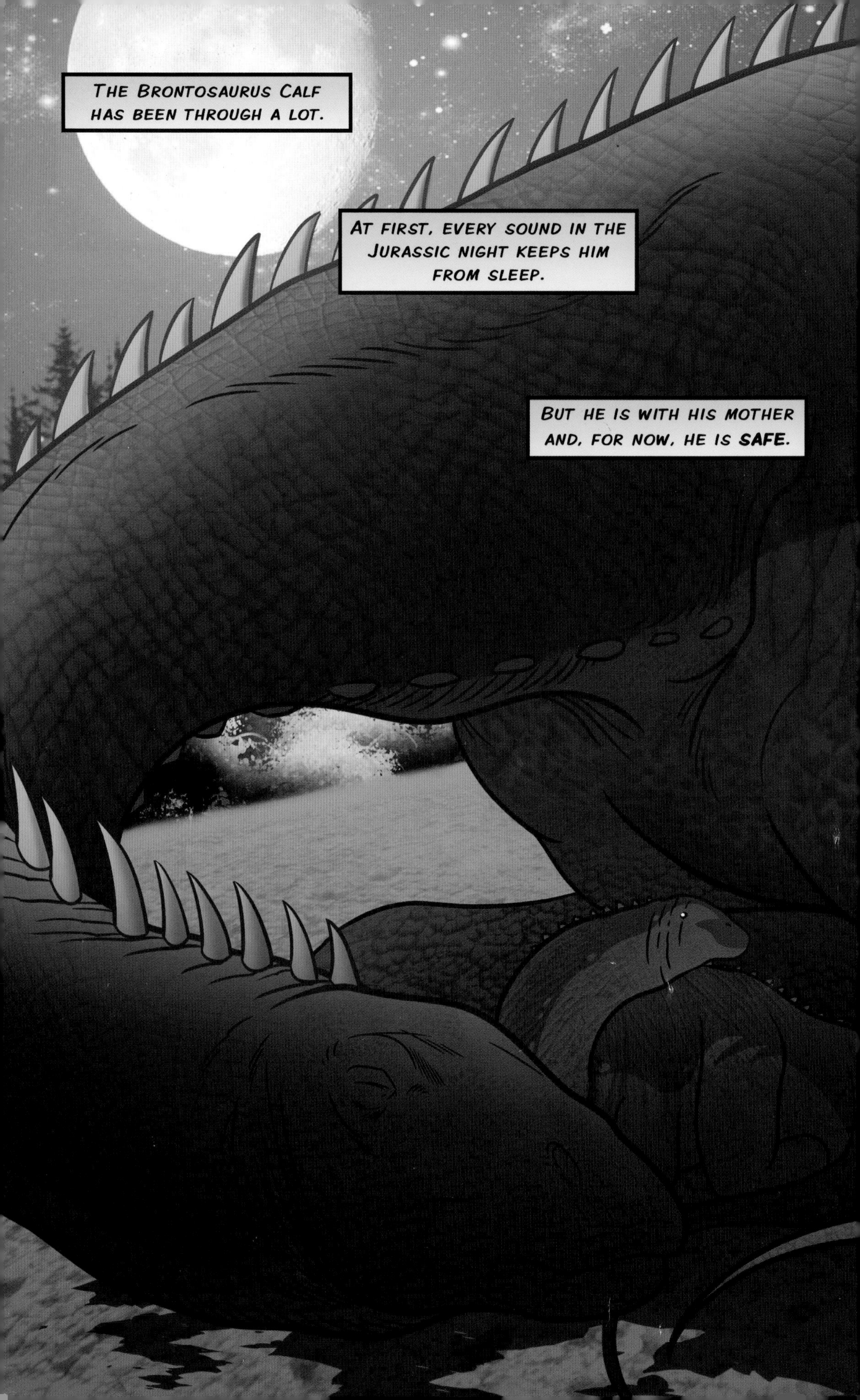
THE BRONTOSAURUS CALF HAS BEEN THROUGH A LOT.
AT FIRST, EVERY SOUND IN THE JURASSIC NIGHT KEEPS HIM FROM SLEEP.
BUT HE IS WITH HIS MOTHER AND, FOR NOW, HE IS SAFE.

HE'S SURVIVED THIS
ADVENTURE –

AND THAT MAKES HIM
STRONGER THAN MOST.

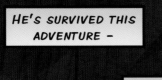

HE JUST MIGHT HAVE WHAT IT
TAKES TO **SURVIVE** TO ADULTHOOD
IN THIS JURASSIC WORLD.

AND IF HE DOES, HE WILL
BECOME A TRUE –

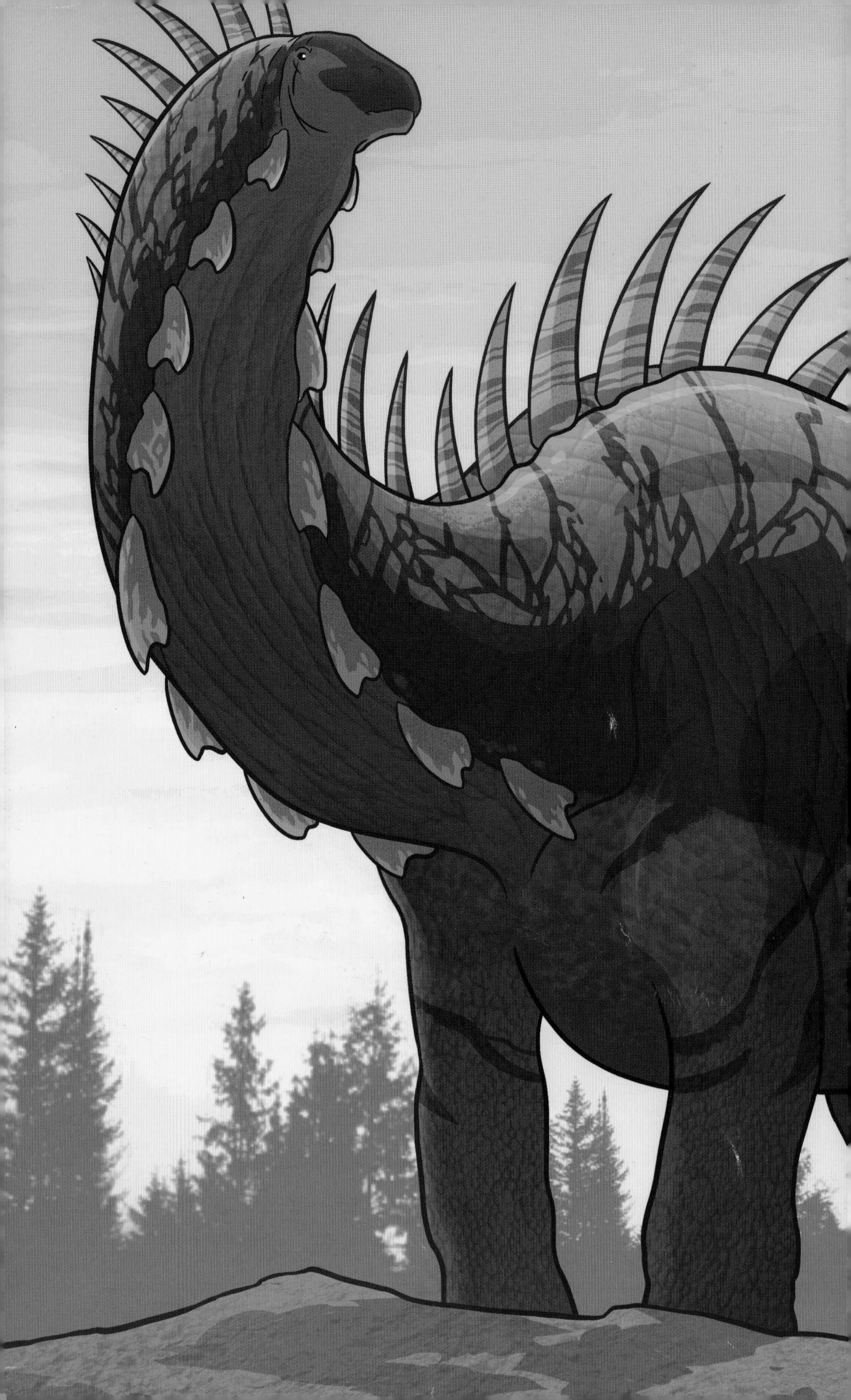

THUNDER LIZARD

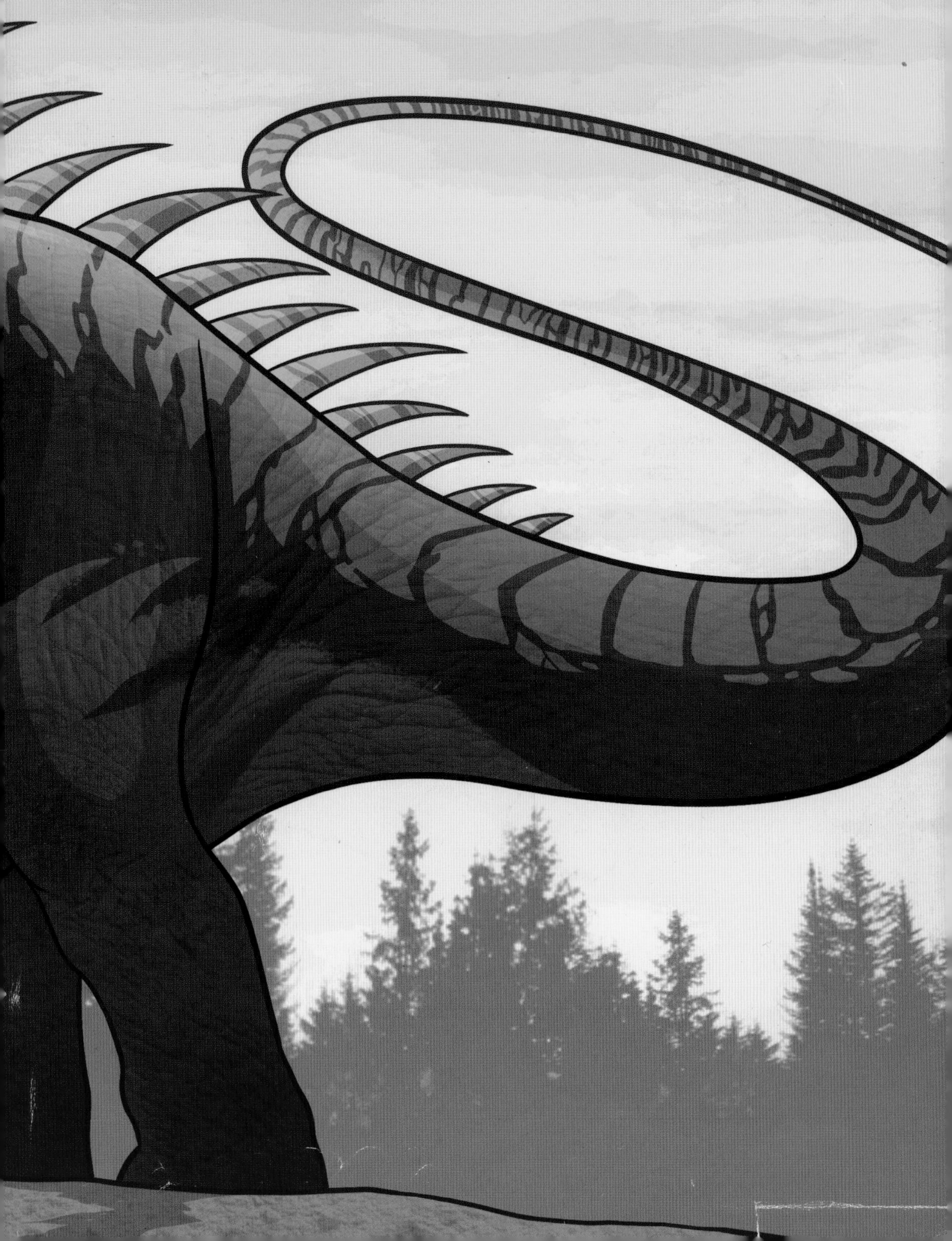

REXTOOTH
STUDIOS
REXTOOTH.COM

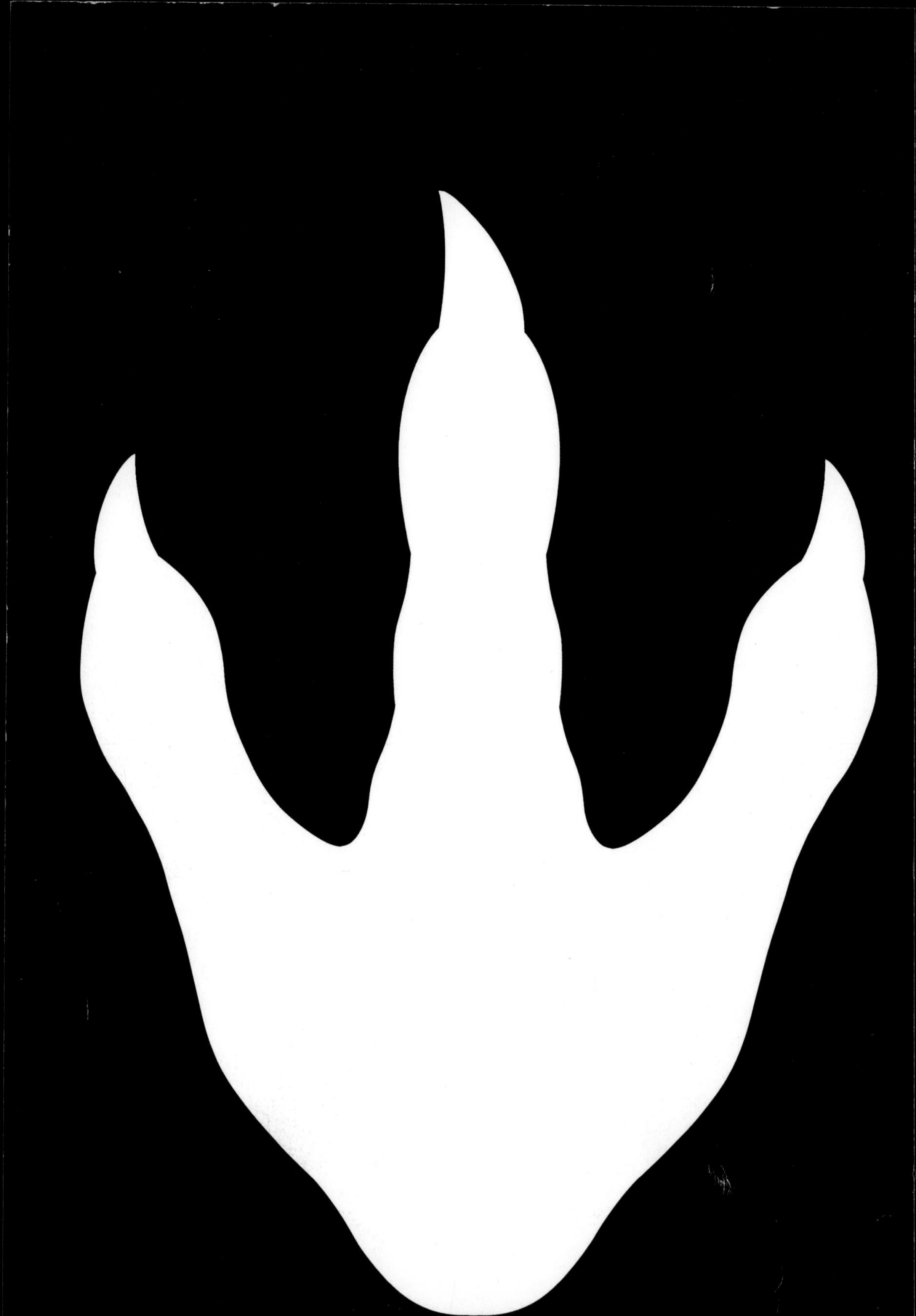